Safe,
Strong,
& Streetwise

Safe, Strong, & Streetwise

by Helen Benedict

Joy Street Books

Little, Brown and Company
Boston   Toronto

FIRST EDITION

The author gratefully acknowledges permission to reprint excerpts
from:
Adolescent Sexuality in Contemporary America, by Robert C. Sorensen.
Copyright © 1972, 1973 by Robert C. Sorensen. Reprinted by
permission of Harry N. Abrams, Inc.
The Silent Children, by Linda T. Sanford. Copyright © 1980 by Linda
Tschirhart Sanford. Reprinted by permission of Doubleday &
Company, Inc.
Men Who Rape, by A. Nicholas Groth with H. Jean Birnbaum.
Copyright © 1979 by Plenum Press. Reprinted by permission.

Library of Congress Cataloging-in-Publication Data

Benedict, Helen.
  Safe, strong, & streetwise.

  "Joy Street Books"
  Summary: Section titles include "Who Would Hurt You
and Why," "Your Sexual Rights and Responsibilities,"
"Protecting Yourself Inside," "Self-Defense," and
"Getting Help." Includes an appendix for parents.
  1. Child molesting — United States — Juvenile liter-
ature. 2. Child molesting — United States — Prevention —
Juvenile literature. [1. Child molesting. 2. Child
molesting — Prevention. 3. Sex crimes — Prevention.
4. Safety] I. Title. II. Title: Safe, strong, and
streetwise.
HQ72.U53B46 1986   362.7'044   86-8002
ISBN 0-316-08899-4 (hc)
ISBN 0-316-08900-1 (pb)

MV

*Published simultaneously in Canada
by Little, Brown & Company (Canada) Limited*

PRINTED IN THE UNITED STATES OF AMERICA

To my son, Simon

Acknowledgments

Thank you to all the teenagers who spoke to me for this book, and to all the adults who recalled past experiences they allowed me to use. Thanks also to Michael Castleman, A. Nicholas Groth, Linda Sanford, Robert Sorensen, Flora Colao, and Tamar Hosansky for the information in their valuable books. Finally, thanks to my husband, Stephen O'Connor, my editor, Melanie Kroupa, and to Trisha Brinkman, for all their help.

Contents

Safe,
Strong,
& Streetwise

Introduction

As a teenager, you are changing from a child to a sexual being. You are on the threshold of the biggest change in your life, for not only do you feel different when you become a sexual being, you are seen as different by the rest of the world.

Becoming a sexual being brings up all kinds of issues — some wonderful, some difficult — and you have a right to know all you can about how to handle your new status. Knowing about the dangers of sex as well as its pleasures will help you develop a happy, healthy, and safe sexual life. It will protect you not only from the misunderstandings that can lead a boyfriend or acquaintance to hurt you, but from the harm anyone might intentionally want to do to you.

The most common types of sexual assault happen almost every day, especially to girls: being jeered at in the street, being touched in a sexual way against your will, seeing a flasher, being felt up by a stranger, being pushed to go too far by a date.

The next most common assault happens when an adult or older teenager, usually someone you know, tries to use your body in a sexual way that you don't like. Recent statistics indicate that a third to a half of all American children, girls *and boys*, are sexually molested in this way before they turn eighteen.

Finally, there is the more remote but nevertheless realistic chance that you might be seriously sexually assaulted or raped. A woman is raped every *six seconds* in this country, and most of those victims are teenage girls. Seven to 10 percent of rape victims are male.

This book will address all these dangers. It will show you how best to protect yourself from strangers, how to recognize and avoid sexual assault by people you know, and how to handle everyday assaults.

As a young teenager, you can have one powerful advantage over the people who try to assault you: knowledge. Assailants pick on you primarily because they expect you to be ignorant, intimidated, and confused about what's happening. They think you won't understand it, won't know what to do, and will be too frightened to resist. When you *do* know what to do, therefore, you can take them completely by surprise. What man, slipping his hand up a young girl's shirt in the bus, expects her to chop his arm away and denounce him to all the other passengers? What camp counselor, attempting to molest a teenage boy, expects him to let out a bloodcurdling self-defense yell? You'll learn here how to do these things and more.

Something else should be mentioned here — the neglect of male victims. The discussion of male sexual assault is still taboo, yet statistics show that young boys are assaulted almost as often as girls, and that teenage boys and adult men can be — and are — sometimes raped. On a recent live radio show in Washington, D.C., a man phoned in to tell me, "I was raped when I was ten by my uncle. I kept it a secret for twenty years. I never dared tell anyone about it because no one ever talked about male rape in those days. I lived a life of self-destruction and drugs, always looking for other people who'd been hurt as much as I was." If the sexual assault of boys had been talked about in those days, that man might have been spared his decades of misery. For this reason, I have addressed this book to both sexes.

I hope that this book will not only make you safer, but will help you feel stronger and braver. One of the most frightening things in the world is feeling helpless. The more you learn about how to protect yourself and about your sexual rights, the less helpless you'll feel. And not feeling helpless means being able to enjoy life — and love — a great deal more.

ONE

Why You Need This Book

> This is depressing. Who wants to think about the
> sick people out there who might want to hurt me?
> I'll just keep away from dangerous places and I'll be
> okay.

Most of us think defensively like this whenever the subject of sexual assault comes up. "If I'm just a little sensible," we tell ourselves, "I won't have to worry about
all the perverts out there looking for victims. I'm a nice
person, and nice people don't get hurt."

If only that were true. Unfortunately, being a "nice"
person does not protect us from becoming the victim
of a crime. Being "just a little sensible" doesn't always
help, either. We are tempted to believe that only people who are delinquent or careless get assaulted, because that makes us feel immune, but the truth is that
criminals rarely care who we are, what we are like, or
how we feel. They don't see our intelligence, looks, or
personality as any kind of magical protection. Their only
concern is that we are available for attack.

In the crime of sexual assault, the selection of victims

is particularly random. A burglar may prefer to rob people who are rich, or who live in a neighborhood he knows, but a rapist only cares about how easily he can get at us. That's why trying to define a typical victim is always so difficult. A victim of sexual assault can be anyone from a two-month-old baby to a woman in her nineties. We can be assaulted whether we are poor or rich, thin or fat, black or white. We can be assaulted regardless of our sex, personality, religion, nationality, background, education, or class. Every one of us is vulnerable to sexual assault.

WHAT SEXUAL ASSAULT IS

Sexual assault is a criminal offense that comes in many forms. It may be as pathetic as a man exposing his penis to kids in a park, or as dangerous as a rape that ends in murder. Sexual assaults include rape, molestation, sexual abuse, and sodomy. You should understand these terms so that you know if you are being assaulted and what to do about it.

Rape happens when a man or boy forces sexual intercourse on someone. That means he puts his penis in the vagina, mouth, or rectum of a girl or boy by using violence, threats, trickery, or bribery. He may threaten to kill the victim with his bare hands or with a weapon, he may beat the victim up or simply use brute force, or he may trick the victim by making threats and promises like these:

> I'll tell your mother that you posed for pornographic pictures. She'll be so upset she might kill herself or kick you out of the house.
> Your father said I could do this to you. He said it'd be good for you.

You know your parents don't love you. I'm the only person who loves you, so you have to do this with me.
I'll buy you all the things you've ever wanted.

Sodomy means oral or anal intercourse — when the penis enters the mouth or rectum. In some states, the definition of rape is limited to a man forcing his penis into a woman's vagina. In those states the rape of males is called sodomy.

Molestation is sexual assault that stops short of actual rape. A molester might touch your genitals, buttocks, or breasts, or make you touch his or hers. He might just make you look at him naked, or force you to let him look at you. He might take photographs of you naked, or make you look at pornographic photographs with him. He might say obscene things to you while he masturbates, or quickly stick a hand inside your clothes when you don't expect it.

Sexual abuse is another term for sexual assault, but it does not usually mean rape.

Most sexual assaults don't go as far as rape. A man sitting next to you in a movie puts his hand on your leg. A friend's brother makes you take your clothes off. A camp counselor kisses you on the mouth. Your father fondles your genitals in bed. A boyfriend forces you to go further than you want. Your uncle puts his hand in your pants while you're sitting on his lap.

If you are a boy, you can be assaulted in the same way as a girl. You can be kissed, hugged, or fondled against your will. You can be forced to take your clothes off, to pose naked for photographs, or to touch an adult's genitals. You can be assaulted by men, women, or other boys. And you can be raped.

Some sexual assaults are so subtle that they are hard to recognize. A friend's mother, for instance, might say that she wants to take nude photographs of you because you're so beautiful. Or a boy might claim that you should make love with him because his other "cool" girlfriends have. Sometimes it's hard to know whether you are really being forced to do these things, and therefore whether you have a right to complain. The best way to clarify any confusion is to examine exactly how you feel about the act you are being asked to do. *If you feel dread, fear or shock, horror, humiliation, disgust, or even just reluctance, you are being assaulted.*

WHY SEXUAL ASSAULT HURTS

Rapists, molesters, incestuous parents, and other sexual offenders always try to justify their behavior so that it doesn't seem criminal or cruel. A typical excuse is, "I haven't done anything wrong. The kid wanted it, and it didn't hurt anyway." This is simply not true. All sexual assaults hurt, physically and emotionally. No one ever wants to be forced into a sexual act.

Whether you are male or female, eleven or twenty, you want to choose when and how to have sexual encounters. The smallest baby cries in rage when someone makes her put on clothes she doesn't like; from the moment we are born, we don't want to have our bodies forced to do things. Your first dignity is your right over your own body.

When someone assaults you sexually, he takes that dignity away. He ignores your feelings and your personality. He hurts you, degrades you, makes you feel small and worthless and full of guilt, and then tries to tell you that you liked it. He makes you feel like seventeen-year-old Karen did when she was raped by a man she'd just met in a park.

When I was raped, I thought I was going to die. I thought the guy was going to kill me. I remember I begged and cried for him not to kill me; that's probably just what he wanted. He dragged me behind some bushes and waved a lead pipe at me and told me to take my clothes off. Then he pushed me on the ground where it was cold and dirty and lay on top of me and had sex with me. He hit me a lot to keep me quiet. I was in pain all over, but none of it was as bad as the fear that he would kill me.

Or like this thirteen-year-old boy felt when he was assaulted by his babysitter.

I was about thirteen and she was eighteen or nineteen. She was babysitting for [me]. I came into the kitchen, and she dragged me into the bedroom. I didn't know what was happening. She pulled down my pants and masturbated me. Then she lay down on the bed and put me on top of her. It was painful. Her pubic hair was sharp, and it felt like spikes were cutting and sticking me. I was shaking and trembling. It scared the hell out of me. I didn't tell anybody about it, but after that, I told my mother I didn't want a babysitter anymore, and I stayed by myself.

Physically, sexual assault can be extremely painful. There is a common myth that rape doesn't actually hurt victims, it just frightens them, but that is not true. Forced sexual intercourse in any circumstance hurts a lot. Some victims say it felt like their skin was being torn apart. Molestation can hurt physically, too, especially if violence is used, for the genital area is tender and vulnerable. But psychologically, the hurt is even worse. Some victims have likened rape to being tortured, for you are both humiliated and hurt at the same time. All victims of sexual assault feel terrified, dirty, ashamed, and worthless. Many are deeply traumatized because they thought they were going to be mutilated or murdered.

Another myth that molesters use to justify their actions is that kids are naturally sexual and like sexual relations with adults. Well, it may be true that you like to be sexual — but only when you want to and when you can choose whom to be sexual with. Child molesters who use this excuse are ignoring the fact that when someone older than you comes along and persuades you to have sex, you don't have a free choice. And when you don't have a choice, that means you are being forced.

However old you are, sex should never make you feel all these negative things. It should make you feel happy and relaxed. Above all, it should make you feel loved. Sex that makes you feel unhappy should never happen. Now you can learn to prevent it.

WHAT YOU ALREADY KNOW

We all know something about how to protect ourselves. Your earliest memories may include being taught not to get into a car with strangers, for instance. You probably also know that you shouldn't walk down dark alleyways at night, or hang out in certain parts of town. But many of us ignore what we already know. And many of us think we know more about self-protection than we really do. Listen to these teenagers, all of whom live in a big city and consider themselves streetwise:

I stay in my neighborhood, where it's safe.
I don't walk around alone at night.
I walk with friends after dark.
I call my mother and tell her where I'm going.

All these precautions are sensible, but they are not enough. It *is* a good idea to stay in a neighborhood you know well, but that doesn't mean you are safe: about a third of all rapes take place in or around the victim's own home. In fact, you should be more cautious near your home, not less. It is also wise to avoid being alone when out at night, to protect yourself against strangers, but that is only half the battle: 60 percent of rapes of adults and 85 percent of sexual assaults on children are committed by someone the victim knows. And letting your mother know where you are is always a good idea, but if you are somewhere unsafe, her knowledge of that might not be able to help you.

The reason most people don't know enough about how to protect themselves is simply that they were never taught. Boys aren't taught because people are too embarrassed to think of them as being in as much danger of sexual assault as girls — boys are supposed to be "tough." And girls aren't taught because girls aren't supposed to be streetwise — that's not "ladylike." In general, a lot of adults don't teach children or teenagers self-protection because they believe that kids should be allowed to be kids, to be kept innocent. Unfortunately, innocent can also mean defenseless. Stereotypes about what boys, girls, or kids are like should never get in the way of learning to be safe. You can learn to protect yourself without losing your idealism, your joy, or your freedom.

WHAT YOU CAN DO ABOUT ASSAULTS

The best way to prevent sexual assaults would be to rid people of the drive to commit them. Unfortunately, that isn't so easy. It means changing the circumstances that turn people into molesters; catching those who do it and changing their personalities so they don't need to do it anymore. There are organizations trying to do just that, but it's a long, discouraging process. In the meantime, the next best way to stop assaults is to learn how to protect yourself from them. No method is going to be perfect — even self-defense experts get assaulted sometimes — but the more of us who know how to protect ourselves, the fewer easy victims there will be.

Because you are young, you already have an advantage over many would-be offenders: surprise. One of the main reasons offenders pick on children and teenagers is because they don't expect any resistance; they see you as an easy target. If you know how to outwit an assailant, how to escape, and how to defend yourself, you may be able to catch your attacker off guard and get away. Take the example of Christine, a twelve-year-old Girl Scout who had taken a course in self-defense.

> I was on a crowded bus coming home from school and a man behind me started putting his hand up my shirt. So I yelled, "This man is bothering me!" and chopped his arm away with my hand. He moved away pretty fast. I guess he expected me to just stand there quietly and take it.

Christine was right. Most people who sexually assault teenagers and children do expect you to stand there and take it. And, most of the time, that's exactly what happens. You can change that.

The first way to protect yourself from sexual assault is to learn what it is, why it happens, and how often it happens; in other words, learn to recognize the real dangers and how vulnerable you are to them.

Then you need to learn what your sexual rights are and how to stand up for them. This helps you avoid falling victim to trickery, threats, or your own insecurity.

Next, you have to learn how to be safe outside, at home, at school, and anywhere else you might be. This means not only knowing how to recognize the people, places, and situations that might be dangerous, but knowing how to act like somebody no one would mess with.

Last, but not least, you need to learn actual self-defense. This means learning how to escape from danger *before* anything happens, as well as learning how to actually fight back if you have to.

PROTECTING YOURSELF WITHOUT GETTING PARANOID

One of the most difficult parts of learning self-defense is facing up to your vulnerability without getting frightened or disillusioned. "I don't want to think of the world as evil," you might say. "That just spoils everything." None of us wants to be afraid to go out, afraid to be alone, or afraid to trust others. A lot of us refuse even to think about crime because we don't want our idealistic vision of the world disrupted by fear; we want to think of it as a beautiful, safe place.

Learning to protect yourself against crime *can* make you feel paranoid for a while, especially at first. Many adults and kids taking self-defense classes report feeling more scared than ever for the first week or two. But that soon passes. Protecting your sexual rights doesn't mean never having fun, never relaxing, or never forgetting that crime happens and might happen to you. Self-protection teaches you to exercise better judgment so that, once it has become natural to you, you feel stronger and freer than ever. Elly, who is eleven, found

this out after she took a self-defense course from Girl
Scouts.

Before I took the class, I was once in a movie theater with a friend when a guy next to me put his arm
on my leg and pulled up my skirt. I hit his arm but
he didn't stop. I was so scared I froze. If I'd taken
self-defense then, I'd have known to yell and get
attention, or to run off. Now I have taken the class,
I don't feel so scared. I feel like I know what to do
now.

TWO

Who Would Hurt You and Why

The common image of a rapist is a drooling lunatic who creeps around alleyways. The common image of a child molester is a dirty old man. These images are utterly inaccurate, for most sexual offenders look and act perfectly normal, at least on the outside. In order to protect yourself, you have to understand who offenders are and what motivates them. Understanding them helps you to avoid them.

The types of people who might sexually assault you fall into these major categories:

Rapists or would-be rapists who assault whomever they can, regardless of the victim's age. Some of these offenders assault one sex only, some both.

Child molesters.

Men and women who assault only members of their own family.

Boys who assault their girlfriends or dates.

Some of these offenders are your age, some are older. Some seem respectable, some are already criminals. Some may even have authority over you. They can be teachers, parents, cousins, counselors, clergymen, doctors, older brothers and sisters, neighbors, or friends. The one thing they all have in common is that they don't see you as a person with your own likes, dislikes, and rights. They see you as an object to use the way they want. As one forty-year-old offender said,

> Why should I think about other people's feelings? Who ever thought anything about me? If I need something — well, that's all I need to know. I just go ahead and take it.

WHY SEXUAL ASSAULT HAPPENS

> My friend was walking down a street one day when some old man pulled her into a building and masturbated in front of her. But she was just dumb and young.

When fifteen-year-old Krissy says here that her friend is "dumb and young," what she is really saying is, "I'm not like that, so it won't happen to me." Like most of us, she wants to blame the assault on the victim because that makes *her* feel safer. "It happened to her because she took a stupid risk," we tell ourselves, meaning that *we* know better than to take such a risk. Or we say, "He was asking for it because he hangs out with a bad crowd," meaning that because *we* don't hang out with a bad crowd, we are safe. The trouble is, blaming the victim doesn't really make us safer at all. It does just the opposite, for once we think we're invulnerable, we stop watching out for ourselves.

Sexual assault never happens because of what the victim said or did. Usually, the victim wasn't even taking a risk; he was just going about his normal business. But even if he did take a risk — he walked home late by himself, he didn't look behind him when he opened his door — the assault is not his fault. Nor is it his fault if he broke a rule or acted foolishly. When we take a risk, we do it in the hope that we won't get hurt, not that we will. When we do something careless, we are merely forgetting to consider our safety. And even when we do something "bad," we usually figure we can get away with it. None of these acts mean we are asking to be hurt. That man pulled Krissy's friend in the door simply because she happened to be there, not because of anything she said or did. Blaming her for the assault only adds insult to injury.

Sometimes we take risks because we feel certain that nothing bad can really happen to us. "Bad things only happen to other people," we think. Some people carry this sense of invulnerability to extremes. "If anyone tries to attack me, I'll tell him my mother's sick, then he won't hurt me." "No one would rape a virgin." "I've got cancer. Nothing else bad will happen to me." Unfortunately, rapists don't care about us, our mothers, or our health. In fact, rapists have been known to attack people just because they are helpless from a disease, a handicap, or age; after all, a helpless person is an easy victim.

Sexual assault is caused by only one person: the offender. Why he or she does it is complicated, and some of those reasons will be dealt with in this book. One of the most basic causes of assault, however, is the image of women in our society. From movies to record jackets, women and girls are depicted as sexual objects, as inferior to men, and as people to be used, not respected. A teenage girl poses like a stripper to sell jeans. A half-dressed woman is used to sell cars, whiskey, or cigarettes. Most of the women on record covers are shown with their mouths in sexy pouts and almost nothing on. The songs themselves are full of lyrics like "You belong to me." "The girl is mine." "I'm gonna get her." Sophisticated advertisements suggest that the sign of a successful man is having a fancy car, a diamond tie pin, and a pretty woman, all possessions to show off. Women on TV advertisements either slink around in skin-tight clothes or sit at home babbling about laundry detergents. Pop videos depict women being chased, seduced, manipulated, tied up, and trodden on. Meanwhile, men and boys are presented as playing football, riding horses, making money, and getting women. The idea of women as things to get and men as the ones to get them is so pervasive in all the media that it's hard to think of an exception.

If you are a girl, these stereotyped images teach you that you are worth little unless you are beautiful and sexy, that you have no rights over your own body, and that your highest goal in life should be to catch a man and do his laundry. If you are a boy, the same images teach you that you should chase girls and catch them like rabbits, that girls don't mean it when they say no to sex, and that they're good for nothing but bed and housework. The more we are all bombarded with these images, the more we get the message that women are less than human. With that attitude, sexual assault is easy for men to commit, and hard for women to object to.

On a more individual level, people often sexually assault others because they themselves were assaulted as children. The psychological explanation for this is complex, but it has a lot to do with needing to retrieve the sense of power that the assault took away. When someone is sexually assaulted, his will and sense of control over himself is stolen. Sometimes the only way he feels he can get it back is to repeat what was done to him on another person — usually a person the same age as he was when he was assaulted, this time making himself the attacker instead of the victim.

Other offenders have learned their behavior from watching their mothers being abused. They learn to associate violence with sex until the only kind of sex they can enjoy is sex that hurts someone. Many sexual offenders were so badly abused physically or emotionally as children that they never learned how to respect or love other people. Stopping sexual assault is therefore essential not only to protect young people, but to prevent them from growing up to become offenders themselves.

Here is a list of the types of sexual assault you might experience, and some other reasons why people commit them.

STREET HARASSMENT

Almost every girl and woman in this society has been yelled at in the street by a man. It happens to boys sometimes, too, but mostly it's a phenomenon directed by men at women. See how familiar these taunts sound to you.

Hey, baby, ain't you gonna give me a smile?
What a pair of legs/tits/boobs!
What a piece of ass!

And, once you've walked by pretending to ignore those remarks, how familiar are these ensuing jeers?

What's the matter, you can't smile?
Too stuck up to say hello, huh?
Ah, you're ugly anyway.

Harassing women and girls in this way is such popular entertainment that there probably isn't a single boy reading this book who hasn't either seen friends do it, or done it himself. "Why not?" you might say. "It's only in fun. Anyway, the girls like it. It flatters them." But have you ever really stopped to think what it means or how you would feel if it happened to you? Imagine what it would be like to be walking down the street, wrapped up in your own private thoughts, when a stranger suddenly screams at you, "Hey, you got nice buns!" Imagine how it would feel to be unable to go outside without getting jeered at.

To test out the popular belief that girls are flattered when men shout at them in the street, I asked a number of women and girls how it makes them feel. Here are some of their answers.

It makes me scared to walk past groups of guys on the street.

It makes me real self-conscious. Seeing a guy look at me as if I'm a cow is humiliating.

It makes me so mad I want to kill. I get fantasies of having some magic weapon that'll make them double up in pain as soon as they say anything to me.

Shouting at girls is, in fact, an act of hostility. You wouldn't shout sexual remarks at someone you love or respect — at your mother, sister, girlfriend, or your father, for that matter. Men and boys shout at women because they think that to treat women as objects is "cool," and that it gives them the upper hand.

Harassing women and girls on the street is not only an immature way that men and boys show off to each other, it's a way they vent their hostility toward women without risking their own safety. Often, this hostility stems from feelings of fear or confusion about women. Some men say they resent women just because they are attracted to them: they resent the power women have over them in being desirable. Sometimes a man will harass women as an expression of his own insecurity — dislike for himself, perhaps, and an ability to believe that any female could really like him. Other times the hostility is based on race or class: construction workers, for example, seem to enjoy harassing women dressed in office clothing. The hostility can be disguised as flattery, but often it's right out there in the open, as Hannah found out when she was fourteen.

> It was a school day at lunchtime, and I was walking up to the corner to buy some yogurt. I had to walk past a bunch of construction workers, who were all sitting on the sidewalk eating their lunch. I felt nervous as soon as I saw them, but I didn't want to look stupid and cross the street. One of them shouted, "Look at that ugly chick," and then he lay down on the sidewalk and rolled over to lie at my feet. He was looking up my skirt and laughing. I wanted to kick him in the head, but I was too scared and humiliated. For days after that, I hated myself for not having kicked him.

The message in street harassment to women is this: "I don't respect you. You are nothing but a body to me. And if I want you, I can get you."

FLASHING

Young people, especially girls, are often the target of exhibitionism, or flashing — when a man exposes his genitals or masturbates in public.

> When I was thirteen, I was walking with my class back from the football field to school, when a man shouted. We all turned to look and he was standing in the road masturbating in front of everybody. My teacher got real embarrassed and made us look the other way, but that guy had the whole class freaked out.

Exhibitionists do this on buses, trains, in parks and on street corners — wherever they can get away with it. Psychologists say that flashers get their pleasure from the look of horror on the victim's face, by imagining that their victim is interested in or impressed by their genitals, or by pretending that they are educating a young victim. Some even fantasize that they are having a sexual relationship with their victim, or that they are raping her. Contrary to popular belief, exhibitionists are hardly ever senile old men in raincoats — they can be young boys, as well as adults of all ages and types. Most are not only exhibitionists, they are also child molesters or rapists. Whether they actually go on to touch anyone or not, however, their behavior is far from harmless. Anyone who gets turned on by scaring people is dangerous.

MOLESTING

Child molesters don't restrict themselves to kids under twelve, as many believe. Some exclusively pick on young teenagers. The word "molester" is used rather than "rapist" because this type of offender usually stops short of forcing actual sexual intercourse. A few molesters aren't content with forcing some type of sexual behavior on you, however; they want to beat, torture, or kill you, too. Luckily, this last type of offender seems to be quite rare.

Molesters don't attack kids out of sexual frustration — many of them have wives or girlfriends. Nor are they usually gay men, as is commonly thought. Most are heterosexual or bisexual in their adult preferences. Molesters attack kids because they are thrilled by the chance to have someone helplessly in their power. For them, dominating a child has a sexual thrill.

One type of molester is known as a pedophile (PEDo-file). This person, usually male, is obsessively attracted to children. Pedophiles usually only like children of a specific age. Some only pick on one sex, others will molest both.

Pedophiles often initiate their "relationships" by befriending their victim. They spot someone who looks lonely, neglected, or friendless and start being nice to him; they take him places, give him presents, talk and listen to him, spend time with him. Then, gradually, they begin to make sexual advances. If the pedophile has chosen his victim well — a child who quickly becomes dependent on him for drugs, money, food, or love — he knows the child won't refuse sex. A pedophile often persuades himself and his victim that he loves him or her, but as soon as the victim gets too old for his taste, the pedophile's "love" ends. One convicted pedophile once said that the best way parents can protect their kids from being sexually molested is to love them.

If the child tries to resist, the pedophile might say something like:

> If you tell on me, I'll go to jail. Do you want to do that to a friend?
> If you tell on me, no one will believe you. After all, I'm a respected adult in this town and you're just a kid.
> If you tell your mother about us, the shock will kill her. You couldn't do that to her, could you?
> If you tell on me, we'll both get into trouble.

Pedophiles are usually young to middle-aged men who appear outwardly normal. Contrary to popular belief, they are not necessarily retarded, insane, senile, or addicted to drugs or drink. Psychologists say that pedophiles have, in a way, never grown up. They cannot get along well with other adults and only feel comfortable with younger people who don't threaten or compete with them. Some pedophiles don't or can't have sexual relations with adults at all. Kids make pedophiles feel young again, yet big and powerful at the same time. Also, kids are easy to intimidate into not resisting or reporting the molestation; the pedophile is very wary of getting caught.

Another type of child molester does have regular sexual relations with adults but still assaults kids. He might do it to get back at somebody or some situation he is angry about. He might do it to make himself feel strong and powerful, and he may be violent with his victims. He might do it because he gets a kick out of hurting or dominating someone, and kids are easier to dominate and entrap than adults. As a twenty-nine-year-old man said about why he attacked a boy of twelve:

> There was less trouble getting ahold of kids. Kids were around and they were easy to get to, and there was less risk of getting hurt myself.

Almost all molesters know the kids they assault. Some — and this is true of female as well as male molesters — only assault children within their own families. Some assault their nieces, nephews, cousins, or grandchildren. Others seek out work with young people in order to gain access to them: they become teachers, scout masters, athletic coaches, Big Brothers, foster parents, camp counselors, and youth organizers. Most adults in these positions are not child molesters, of course, but a frightening number are.

For several reasons, a molester will try to get to know you before he assaults you. He can win your trust so that you won't tell on him; he can gain the trust of your parents or guardians so that no one would believe you if you told what he did; and, most of all, he can establish power and authority over you so that it's more difficult for you to say no.

Child molesters of all types tend to repeat their offenses over and over again. One study of 238 male sex offenders in New York and Memphis found that they had attempted or committed a total of 16,666 acts of child molestation — an average of over sixty-eight molestations each. Some had committed so many they had lost count. Molesters tend to plan out their attacks, and to pick victims with care in order to protect themselves from being caught. Look at how carefully this twenty-eight-year-old offender approached his victims.

> I got busted for molesting these boys on my baseball team. But it wasn't like I was exploiting them. I'd worked with those kids for a full year on nothing but their batting and fielding before I ever molested them. It took me that long before they trusted me and stopped treating me like a tough adult coach.

It's important to remember that molesters don't think what they are doing is wrong. They think it's natural and free. They often pretend that their victims are older psychologically than they really are and that the child wanted the "relationship" and even initiated it. In fact, what usually happens is that the victim is either so desperate for attention or love, or so frightened and bewildered, that he or she can't say no.

RAPE

Rapists are men who like to humiliate and terrify people in the worst possible way: to force sex on them and to threaten them with mutilation or murder if they don't comply.

Some rapists attack out of anger. They pick the nearest convenient victim and rape that person as a kind of punishment, a revenge for whatever they are mad about. Some rapists do it to feel powerful; they want to force someone to do what they say because they find the victim's fear and submission sexually thrilling. Some believe that rape is the only way they'll ever have sex because they don't believe a woman would ever find them attractive. Others cannot enjoy sex unless it is violent. A few are genuine sadists and are turned on by torturing their victims. A lot of rapists are a mixture of these types. What all these men have in common is the inability to see or care about how the victim feels at all.

A rapist can be a thirteen-year-old boy or a forty-seven-year-old man. He can be a burglar who crawled through your window. He can be a mugger or your local police chief. He can be your boyfriend. He can be your best friend's father — or even your own.

WHY A PARENT MIGHT ASSAULT YOU

As mentioned earlier, the majority of people who assault the young *know their victims*. No one knows you better than your parents. When a parent sexually assaults you, it's called incest.

Incest can be committed by siblings or mothers, but by far the most common form is between father and daughter. Most of the motivations a father will have for assaulting his daughter are the same as those described for all molesters, but there are some differences. Some fathers, for instance, do it because they believe a daughter is her father's property, and he has a right to do whatever he wants with her body. Some fathers go so far as to think it's their job to introduce their daughters to sex. Other fathers believe they've fallen in love with their daughters, and try to make them into substitute wives. None of these fathers recognize that their daughters are independent human beings, not possessions, and that every girl has a right to choose her own sexual partner, a right to wait until she's ready before she starts sex, and a right to look for her partner outside her home.

Parents sometimes sexually assault their sons. Occasionally, this is done for revenge. One father who raped his twelve-year-old son said he did it to make his wife stay home from work. A mother who sexually assaulted her sons said she did so because they were the only males she could have power over — adult men always beat her up. Some parents do it because their parents did it to them. The reasons and excuses are many, but none of them justify the devastating effect incest can have on the victim.

Stepparents may commit incest, too. Incest used to be defined as something that can only happen between people related by blood, but this is no longer so. The factor that distinguishes parental incest from other sexual assaults, and that makes it especially traumatic for the victim, is that you have been forced into sex by someone on whom you are dependent for care and a home, who has legal authority over you, and whom you probably even love. Step, foster, and adoptive parents — as well as natural parents — have this kind of threefold power over you.

When a parent engages you in any kind of sexual activity, he or she is betraying the basic role of parents: to protect you. It is biologically and emotionally unnatural to have sex with one's child. It is also an infringement on your rights as a human being and on your chances of happiness. What is more, it's illegal. There are ways to stop incest, however. These are discussed in chapters six and eight.

WHY BOYS DATE-RAPE

Many hundreds of thousands of girls have found themselves being forced into some kind of sexual activity by a boyfriend, date, or a boy they have just met.

> I went to a party with a blind date arranged by a friend. When it was over, my date offered to drive me home. We started going in the wrong direction, so I asked him what he was doing. He said he was taking me back to a friend's place to hear some music. When we got there, no one was home. He jumped on me and began kissing me and fooling around. I tried to leave, but he locked the door.
>
> We were in a part of town I didn't know. I didn't know how to get home, and it was late. It was clear that he wasn't going to let me go, and I was scared of him. So I said, "Okay, let's just do it." I couldn't even speak I was so angry — with him, with myself, with the whole situation. I felt awful.

Sexual assault by a boy you know can take many forms, from the obvious rape described above, committed with threats and physical force, to a kind that's so subtle you're not sure whether it's force or seduction. The boy might suddenly jump on you the minute you are alone, like the guy did above, or he might try some of these kinds of threats:

> If you don't do it, I'll tell everyone you did anyway.
> If you don't do it, I'll get your little sister/best friend instead.
> If you don't do it, I'll leave you.

He might try to force you with insults:

You're a whore anyway.
You're frigid.
You think you're too good.

He might try to pressure you with emotional black-mail:

If you love me, you'll do it.
Don't you like me or something?
Everyone else does it.
You're not scared of me, are you?
If you refuse me, I'll hurt myself.

Or, he might simply refuse to take no for an answer.

You're just saying no 'cause girls are supposed to.

Whether the boy is trying to pressure you to have sexual intercourse or to just make you touch his body or let him touch yours, as long as it's against your will, it's sexual assault. It can happen at a party, in your house when your parents are out, at school — wherever he can get you alone. What is more, the boy will probably think he hasn't done anything wrong.

There are a lot of destructive myths in our society that actually encourage boys to force girls into sexual acts. One myth tells us that girls never like sex, so have to be pushed into it. Another myth claims that a girl owes a boy sex if he takes her out, spends money on her, or makes out with her. An especially widespread myth is that girls always say no to sex but never mean it. If a boy is heavily exposed to these sorts of myths without correction, he may learn to be so selfish about sex that he thinks only about what he wants, not any-one else. He may learn, like this young man quoted below — who raped and seriously beat a woman on their second date — that he has a right to "take" a woman's body whenever he wants to.

I think I was really pissed off at her because it didn't go as planned. I could have been with someone else, she led me on but wouldn't deliver . . . I have a male ego that must be fed.

The "reasons" why boys commit sexual assault are complex, but it is important for everyone to understand them in order to prevent sexual assault. They will be discussed in more detail in the next chapter.

WHY BOYS GANG-RAPE

Most group rapes are committed by teenage boys. They usually attack a girl their own age, but occasionally they pick on a boy. They do it to show off to each other, to follow the crowd, to make themselves look tough and dangerous, and because, like all sexual offenders, they don't see their victims as human. Usually a gang rape is instigated by the leader of the group, and the others follow along because they are afraid to look chicken or unmasculine. In a way, gang rape is an extension of the way men and boys harass women in the street: they are behaving like pack animals hunting prey.

THREE

Your Sexual Rights and Responsibilities

The essence of knowing how to protect yourself is knowing the rights and responsibilities that go along with being a sexual person. These apply to all forms of sex, from kissing to sexual intercourse. You need to know your sexual rights no matter how much or little experience you've had, because knowing them helps you to recognize, prevent, and avoid all kinds of sexual assault. You need to know your sexual responsibilities so that you can avoid hurting other people. Most important of all, knowing your sexual rights and responsibilities helps you to enjoy sex in the best way possible.

YOUR SEXUAL RIGHTS

1. YOU HAVE A RIGHT TO ENJOY SEX.
2. YOU HAVE A RIGHT TO WAIT UNTIL YOU'RE READY FOR SEX.
3. YOU ALWAYS HAVE A RIGHT TO SAY NO.
4. YOU HAVE A RIGHT TO BE RESPECTED.
5. YOU HAVE A RIGHT TO SAY YES TO SOME SEXUAL ACTIVITIES AND NO TO OTHERS.

6. YOU HAVE A RIGHT TO HAVE ANY SEXUAL FANTA-
SIES YOU WANT.

YOU HAVE A RIGHT TO ENJOY SEX

When there's a lot of talk about sexual assault, it's
sometimes hard to remember that sex itself is a beautiful, natural experience, or it should be. It should make
you feel like this girl did when she made love with her
boyfriend:

> What were my feelings? I don't know how to ex-
> plain them except that they were warm feelings.
> Physically close feelings. There's just something
> about him that is just shining out bright. . . . When
> he began to touch me, that first time I just got chills
> and quivers and all that stuff through my body . . .
> I never wanted to [quit]. Just go on forever. We don't
> talk to each other; we just look at each other. We
> don't have to talk.

YOU HAVE A RIGHT TO WAIT UNTIL YOU'RE
READY FOR SEX

One of the main ways to guarantee that you will enjoy sex is to wait until you're ready before you begin
having it. Don't make yourself start sex before you really
want to just to please a partner or keep up with the
crowd. Here is the testimony of a fourteen-year-old girl
who let this happen to her.

> I forced myself not to feel [bad] when they touched
> me, because I feared I was frigid or weird or some-
> thing like that. So I gritted my teeth. I didn't dislike
> what they were doing, but it was the way they made
> me feel while they were doing it. Like that's what

made me stop. You know, I'd start thinking this is really disgusting.

"How will I know when I'm ready?" you might ask. Well, if the idea of sex frightens or disgusts you, you aren't ready yet and you aren't going to be able to enjoy it. If you feel unmistakable desire and eagerness, however, and you aren't frightened by sex, you probably are ready.

The main reason people make love or make out before they are ready is because they think their partner expects it.

When I was sixteen, I had a boyfriend who wanted to make love all the time. Sometimes I was in the mood, but on the whole I didn't like it very much. After a while, I came to dread being with him. I took drugs in the hope they'd help me like it better, but instead I became more and more sick of it. I never thought of complaining because I didn't want to seem frigid, and I thought, since he was a boy, he needed it. The weird thing is that, when I met him again years later, he told me he was embarrassed about our lovemaking back in those years. He said, "I didn't know what I was doing then. I couldn't have given you much pleasure."

Misunderstandings like this happen between couples because of the myths about the way males and females behave. Boys, it is believed, always want sex no matter what: they're always ready for it, always eager, and always horny. Because of this myth, boys often think they've got to initiate sex and follow it through whenever they have the chance, even if they don't feel like it. And girls think they'd better please the boy or else they'll be torturing him.

Girls, on the other hand, are believed to either never want sex or to always pretend they don't want it. Movies often show women moaning, "No, no," as they swoon into the arms of a seducer. This myth makes boys think they have to pressure the girl, and that when she says no, she's only acting.

The truth is that boys, as much as girls, can be scared by sex. They might be afraid because they don't think they're very good at it yet, and they fear the girl will laugh at them. They might not feel emotionally ready for sex yet, or not be attracted enough to the girl. Or they might be afraid that something will go wrong, like ejaculating too early, not getting an erection, or not satisfying the girl. If you, as a boy, don't feel like having sex, don't scold yourself for being abnormal — you're not.

The truth about girls is that they do, of course, like making love, but often not until they are somewhat older than the age at which boys are ready. Also, girls usually prefer to trust and like the boy they make love with. When a girl says yes, she means it; when she says no, she means that, too. A girl who likes a boy enough to want to make some form of love with him isn't about to risk losing him by pretending to reject him. If you, as a girl, fear that not being ready means you're frigid or unsexual, don't worry. You're just young.

Both sexes will have a healthier sex life if they don't push themselves too soon.

YOU ALWAYS HAVE A RIGHT TO SAY NO

Susie's father said to her, "I made you, so you belong to me. You have to do what I want." He forced sex on her from age ten to thirteen and she thought she had no right to say no.

If a person with authority over you, like a teacher or a parent, tries to order you to have sex, you have an absolute right to refuse. You don't belong to anyone else — not a parent, not a boyfriend or girlfriend, not any authority figure, not anyone who loves you, not anyone you love. Human bodies cannot be owned. The days of slavery are over.

If a boyfriend tries to pressure you to have sex against your will in the name of "love," you also have a right to say no.

> One of my first boyfriends used to give me a real hard time about making love with him every time he saw me. He said his previous girlfriend had slept with him and that if I loved him, I'd sleep with him too. But I was only fifteen and I didn't really trust him enough. Plus, I was too scared.

Anyone who pressures you to have sex in the name of love should be told that that isn't love, that's pure selfishness.

Your right to say no never changes, no matter what the circumstances. If you've broken a rule, like going out with a person your parents disapprove of, or you've been stupid, cruel, careless, or even criminal, no one has a right to punish you by making you have sex. If someone's spent money on you, taken you out, or given you presents, you don't owe him even as much as a kiss. Even if you've promised to make love and then changed your mind, you have a right to say no. Your body is not a bargaining chip and you are not for sale.

YOU HAVE A RIGHT TO BE RESPECTED

I know a guy who loses respect for a girl as soon as she's slept with him. I see him fall in love and idealize these girls, but as soon as they became his

girlfriend, he starts treating them with such con-
tempt it's embarrassing to be around them. He tried
to go out with me, but I told him, "I think we'd
work better as just friends." Now he treats me better than any of his girlfriends.

There is still a double standard in this country about
boys, girls, and sex. A boy who is sexually active early
or who has many girlfriends is admired — he's seen as
"cool" and sexy. A girl who behaves the same way is
looked down upon, considered "loose." But girls have
as much right as boys to be sexually active. No one
should tell you he doesn't respect you because of your
sexual activities, or pressure you because of them. A
boy who says, "You did it with him, so why not with
me?" should be told to get lost.

There is another double standard in this country, too:
a young person's right to choose isn't respected as much
as an adult's. Molesters use this double standard to force
sex on kids. They interfere with your right to choose
by telling you that you don't know your own mind or
that you don't understand your own desires. They tell
you that you have to do what they say because they
have authority over you and your body. They even say
that you have to do what they want for "your own good."
All this is nonsense. Your choice over what to do with
your body should be respected as much as an adult's.

YOU HAVE A RIGHT TO SAY YES TO SOME
SEXUAL ACTIVITIES AND NO TO OTHERS

Just because you've become physically intimate with
someone doesn't mean you have to do anything you
don't want. If you've almost gone all the way but haven't,
you aren't obliged to. If you've made love with someone before, you aren't obliged to do so again. If you

are willing to engage in some types of sexual activities but not others, you have a right to say so. If a boy tells you that you've gone too far to stop, that he'll explode or turn blue, don't believe him. Being frustrated might be unpleasant, but it won't hurt him.

This applies to boys, too, for sometimes girls will pressure them into making love when they don't want to. For boys it can be especially difficult to refuse because you know you are supposed to be ready for sex whenever the opportunity arises; it isn't "cool" to enjoy kissing but not to want to make love. But you have as much right as anyone to set limits, to stop when you want and refuse what you want.

If you like making out with your partner but you don't want to go any farther yet, say something like "It's not that I don't like you, I do. I'm just not ready to do any more yet."

YOU HAVE A RIGHT TO HAVE ANY SEXUAL FANTASIES YOU WANT

Adults and teenagers who've been assaulted sometimes blame themselves because of the sexual fantasies they've had while daydreaming or masturbating: they are ashamed of them and think they're being punished for them. But you have a right to have any sexual fantasies you want without guilt. A lot of people feel especially guilty for having fantasies of rape or punishment, or for having sexual fantasies about people other than their boyfriend or girlfriend. Yet, fantasies like this are normal — everyone has them. Also, fantasizing something doesn't mean you really want it to happen. Some psychologists believe that people who fantasize about rape, for example, really want to be raped. But there's a big difference, for in fantasy, you are in control because you are making up the story. In a rape, the rapist is in control. In a fantasy, you feel desire. In a rape, you feel terror. In a fantasy, you are not in fear for your life. In a rape, you think you are going to be murdered. Your fantasies are your private affair and have nothing to do with any assailant's need to hurt.

YOUR SEXUAL RESPONSIBILITIES

1. YOU SHOULD ALWAYS CONSIDER THE FEELINGS OF YOUR PARTNER.
2. YOU SHOULD NEVER PRESSURE SOMEONE TO HAVE SEX.
3. YOU SHOULD RESPECT YOUR PARTNER.
4. SEX SHOULD BE A MUTUAL PLEASURE, NEVER A PUNISHMENT.
5. YOU SHOULD SHARE RESPONSIBILITY FOR BIRTH CONTROL AND SEXUAL HEALTH WITH YOUR PARTNER.

YOU SHOULD ALWAYS CONSIDER THE FEELINGS OF YOUR PARTNER

The key to happy lovemaking is considering the feelings of your partner. When you are sensitive to his or her moods, likes, and dislikes, you can help build trust and relaxation between you — and that's good for being in love and making love. So if your partner is upset about something and wants to talk rather than make out, you should put your own needs aside for the moment and tend to his or hers.

YOU SHOULD NEVER PRESSURE SOMEONE TO HAVE SEX

Pressuring someone to have sex is a losing game because pressure is never going to create desire where there wasn't any before. What's more, even when people do succumb to pressure, they are succumbing against their will. That's assault.

> I was really timid and so [my boyfriends] would usually use force — I mean they wouldn't force it, but they would use words with force in them. Like if it was my boyfriend he'd say, "I'm going to leave you if you don't" and "This is what I really want. You've got to make me feel good." So I'd usually end up losing the guy.

If you are a boy, you should never act like this sixteen-year-old's boyfriends. Even if you genuinely think a girl intends to make love and are surprised when she won't, you shouldn't pressure her. Phrases like "Don't be a prude," "You agreed to go out with me, so what did you expect?" and "Why did you invite me over if you didn't want to do this?" are really translations of "If you don't let me kiss/feel/make love to you, you are a jerk." Everyone has a right to say no without being made to feel like a jerk.

Instead of trying to persuade a reluctant girl to make some kind of love with you, you should ask yourself a few questions: "Why does she need persuading? Don't I turn her on? What would she like me to do? Doesn't she like me? Is she afraid?" You would build up a much better relationship with her if you found out the answers to some of these questions instead of pressuring her.

There are other kinds of pressures that both sexes

sometimes use to force a person to have sex, too, and these are equally important to avoid: being more popular at school, being older, being richer, having more experience, or having authority over someone. Even if a person is big and strong, he can, like the boy quoted below, be intimidated by these sorts of advantages into unwanted sex. This boy was so frightened by the girl's odd behavior, and so awed by her superior age and experience, that he was afraid to say no.

> I got aware of sex when I was thirteen or fourteen from *Playboy* and magazines like that. But when it actually happened to me in bed, I was more or less raped. My mom had a friend over and she brought her daughter. Her daughter was an insane type . . . she got mad and went out in the garden and took a bottle of vodka and drank the whole thing. . . . And then she came up to my room and she started doing this whole number on me . . . I was really scared. I was petrified. I almost wanted to cry. She just started talking to me and all those other things, and we just had sex. It was always something I wanted to do, but I wanted to back out at the last minute with her . . .

To use any kind of advantage or pressure to force a person to have sex is assault.

YOU SHOULD RESPECT YOUR PARTNER

Sex can make you feel vulnerable, especially when you're new at it. Even just kissing or making out can make you feel that way. You've never been that physically close to anyone before, and you've rarely been that emotionally exposed, either. That is why good sexual relations require trust between the partners. If a boy or girl has told you secrets, declared love for you, or made some kind of love with you, you should never make fun of him or her for it. When people have been intimate with you like that, they have made themselves vulnerable to you. Don't betray them.

SEX SHOULD BE A MUTUAL PLEASURE, NEVER A PUNISHMENT

There are various ways in which men and women of all ages use sex inappropriately in this society. At one extreme is rape, when a man literally uses sex as an instrument of punishment and torture. On a more everyday level, both sexes sometimes use their sexual hold over someone to play power games. A girl might refuse to make out with her boyfriend one night until he says he loves her, for instance. By doing this, she's using sex as a reward for something she forced out of him, and she's using the withholding of sex as a punishment. This is neither honest nor fair. A boy might do the same sort of thing, or he might force sex on a girl as a way of degrading her because he's mad at her or jealous. Using sex to manipulate people cheapens the act, ruins the pleasure, and destroys the chance of a good, loving relationship.

YOU SHOULD SHARE RESPONSIBILITY FOR BIRTH CONTROL AND SEXUAL HEALTH WITH YOUR PARTNER

This subject may seem not to belong in a book about sexual assault, but it does. Part of respecting someone and being considerate of his or her feelings — the enemies of sexual assault — is being concerned over the consequences of your sexual relationship together. With sexual diseases on the increase, every person has a right to know if his or her partner is healthy. Equally important, the responsibility for birth control belongs to *both* partners.

FOUR

Protecting Yourself among People

You've already completed the first steps toward becoming the kind of person no one would mess with by facing the realities of sexual assault and becoming aware of your sexual rights. The next step is learning how to protect yourself during your daily life: with the people you know, on dates, at parties, out on the street, in public places like school or a park, and at home. None of the suggestions in the next four chapters are guaranteed to make you 100 percent safe — nothing can — but they should make you less vulnerable.

Because you are much more likely to be sexually assaulted by someone you know than by a complete stranger, the first thing to learn is how to protect yourself on dates, at parties, on jobs, and in other social situations. These guidelines can help you become safer and freer to enjoy yourself without fear.

• *Decide right now what kind of intimacy you want with the people in your life.* Don't leave the decision until the moment someone makes a move toward you; it's harder to resist when you have to decide on the spot. Start with the adults you know. Which ones do you like to hug you and which not? Which ones don't you like to be touched by in any way? Do you mind being kissed on the mouth by any of them or not? Do you let any adults kiss, touch, or hug you even though you don't like it? If so, ask yourself why. Consider stopping them by insisting on shaking hands instead, or by just backing away. Kids are taught from an early age to put up with being pawed by adults. But you are old enough now not to have to tolerate it anymore.

Now think about the person you are dating, or would like to be dating. How much do you want to be touched by him or her? If you can figure out your limits now, when you are alone and able to think calmly, you can make those limits clear when you have to.

Finally, think about your friends of both sexes. How much touching do you like to do with them? Are you comfortable with a lot of hugs and kisses and pats on the back, or do you prefer to be touched only by people you love? Remember, you have a right to determine who touches you and who doesn't.

• *Ask yourself if there is anyone you know right now who makes you uncomfortable.* Is there someone who touches you too often, puts his or her hand on you, or always insists on kissing you hello even when you try to back off? Is there someone who always stands too close to you, or tries to get you to tell him or her intimate secrets about your life? Is there someone who likes to tease you or to make you embarrassed or uneasy? Here are the danger signs of a potential assailant:

1. The person keeps trying to invade your physical or emotional privacy.
2. The person enjoys making you feel stupid or nervous.
3. The person doesn't listen to you or take you seriously, but dismisses you with phrases like "Don't be silly" or "You don't really mean that."

If you can think of anyone like that, decide what you can do about it. Can you keep away from that person? Can you get him or her out of your life? If not, can you make it clear that you don't like what he or she is doing? If you stand up for yourself and say, "Don't put your arm around me, it makes me uncomfortable," or "I'm sorry, but I'm not answering that question," you might be able to stop the behavior. If you like the person, try saying something like "It's not that I don't like you, it's just that I don't like being kissed/hugged/talked to like that." If the person is considerate and really likes you, he or she will stop the behavior, although perhaps not until after a few defensive or angry phrases. But if the person gets angry and stays angry, that's a danger sign, too, for it reveals an unwillingness to care about you.

• *Make a deal with your parents: ask them to pick you up whenever you call them for help, wherever you are, without asking you questions and without getting mad at you.* Even if it's late, you are somewhere you are not supposed to be, and you are drunk or stoned, they should come get you and promise not to get angry or to blame you for your predicament. Most of the time, you probably won't want to involve your parents in what you're doing, but just having them there as a safety valve can make you feel more secure. One mother made an arrangement like this with her teenage daughter:

> If you find yourself with a boyfriend in his house late at night, he's trying to make you have sex when you don't want to and you can't get away, call me and I'll come. I won't embarrass you in front of him and I won't say anything about it for a whole day. Then we can sit down and talk about it.

If your parents won't agree to this arrangement, remind them that your safety should come first over everything. Tell them that a method like this was used in a town where many teenagers had been in drunk-driving accidents. Instead of driving when intoxicated, the teenagers began calling their parents to pick them up. The rate of accidents dropped sharply.

• *Give your parents the appendix of this book to read.* It will show them how to help you be safer without intruding on your life.

DATES

There has been a great deal of talk in the media lately about "date rape" — rape by boyfriends, dates, and male friends. Much of this attention has been focused on how much it happens (a lot) and how it affects the victim (badly). Here you can learn how to prevent it.

• *If you are a girl, be strong in your relationship with boys.* Don't let your date always make the arrangements and decisions about what to do when you go out — assert your own wants. And don't let him do all the paying, either, because that gives him power over you. For instance, if you have a fight with him and want to go home early, but are in the middle of a movie he's paying for, you might feel obliged to stay for fear of being impolite. Paying your own way puts less of a burden on the boy and makes you feel more independent and in control. When you come across as independent, you are less likely to be taken advantage of.

• *If you are a boy, don't feel that in order to be "masculine" you have to make all the decisions and do all the paying.* That idea is outdated and sexist and money shouldn't be part of a dating relationship anyway. When relationships are more equal, both partners are less likely to feel used.

• *If you go out with someone you don't know well, stay in public places for the first few dates.* If you are a girl, you will feel safer this way. If you are a boy, you will have the chance to get to know your date gradually and in a more relaxed way. Some boys think that if a girl agrees to go somewhere with a boy alone, she's agreeing to sex, which isn't necessarily true.

• *Think about what you expect from a dating relationship.* Do you want your boyfriend or girlfriend to also be your best friend? Do you trust him or her? Why or why not? What do you need to happen before you will trust that person? How well do you want to know someone before you start any sexual activity? How do you want to feel about a person before you make love for the first time? What sorts of feelings do you want a person to have about you before you make love for the first time?

Once you know what you really want from a boyfriend or girlfriend, compare that to what you are actually getting. Then decide whether you are making your expectations clear.

• *Decide your sexual limits.* How far are you willing to go sexually right now? A lot of people never really articulate to themselves just how far they really want to go, so they try to decide at the last minute, when it's almost too late.

• *Once you know your limits, stick to them.* Make it clear to your boyfriend or girlfriend from the outset what you will and won't do. If you are a virgin, for instance, and want to stay that way, tell your friend as soon as the relationship gets sexual. If you are a girl and a boy starts doing something you don't want, like putting his hand on your breast, don't let him go ahead in the hope he'll stop there — make him stop right away. You could say, "Let's just kiss, but I don't want to do any more right now." If the boy cares about you and respects your wishes, he will stop. If you are a boy, don't feel you have to press ahead sexually until the girl stops you; ask her how far she wants to go if she won't tell you initially. And think about how far *you* really want to go, too. It's much more pleasant to know what to expect than to be waiting anxiously for her to stop you at any minute.

You might be embarrassed to tell someone what you will or won't do sexually, but it's much worse to end up quarreling over sex. As David, who is sixteen, said, "If girls and boys could be clearer about how far they're willing to go, the whole world would be happier!"

• *Never let anyone force you into being alone with him or her against your will.* Be firm from the start and say, "No thanks, I want to stay with our friends. I'm having fun here," or, "No thanks, I don't want to go there." If the person ignores these refusals and tries to bully you, get away from him or her and think about whether you want to stay with someone that pushy.

• *If you are making out with your partner and the question of having intercourse comes up, remember your sexual rights and don't agree to it if you don't want to.* If your partner says something like "You'd do it if you loved me," your answer could be, "If you loved me, you'd respect my wishes."

• *If you are a girl, don't pretend to reject a boy sexually if you don't mean it.* It confuses a boy, which isn't fair to him, and leads him to believe the myth that women never mean it when they say "no."

• *If you are dating a boy who has a reputation for "scoring," be prepared for him to try to pressure you into sex.*

• *If you are dating a girl who is used to having sex with her boyfriends, don't assume she expects the same from you.* Don't pressure a girl to have sex just because you know she's had it before, and at the same time try not to get hung up about "performing" or being as "good" as her other boyfriends. Making love concerns only the two of you. It should not be a way of competing with other boys.

• *If your boyfriend or girlfriend is old enough to drive, and you like to go "parking," avoid going to isolated areas.* This is for the protection of both of you, because places like lovers' lanes and country fields can be dangerous. Sometimes rapists look for couples in places like this and use the opportunity to tie up the boy and rape the girl, to rape both of you, or assault you both in some other way. Choose an area where lots of couples go parking, or a populated area where you can have both privacy and safety, like down a side street. Leave the key in the ignition so that you can drive away if anything happens, and lock the doors. Put the window up, too, but if you leave the engine on for warmth, *never close the windows all the way* — you'll poison yourselves with carbon monoxide.

HOW TO HANDLE ASSAULT BY A DATE

This section is aimed at girls, for boys are rarely, if ever, assaulted by a girl on a date. Boys are in more danger from gangs of other boys and from older men and women.

Thinking about the possibility of being assaulted by a boy you're going out with is extremely unpleasant: you want and need to trust people that you like. On the whole you can, but if your trust is ever violated, remember: it is not your fault. No one's judgment is perfect enough to foresee all danger. Here's what to do if a date turns assaultive:

• *If a boy wants sex from you and won't take no for an answer, no matter how firm you are, that's assault.* You have a guy on your hands who is so absorbed in himself that he doesn't care at all how you feel. All he wants is to feel powerful through sex, and he's prepared to do anything to feel that, even to use violence. Once you've recognized this, assess the situation. Can you run away or call for help? How far from people are you? Can you attract attention? Can you use the self-defense methods described in chapter seven?

If you can't find an alternative, try to talk your way to safety. Say something like "Look, you don't have to get mad. I want it too, but I need to relax first. I know somewhere more comfortable we could go." Then try to get him back to the party with you, to a friend's house — anywhere public. You could even say you want to eat first, or you need a drink or a cigarette to relax, and you know someone who could get you one. The idea is to make him think you want to have sex with him so that he doesn't force you, and to lure him somewhere public so that you can escape. Put on your act convincingly — he's got to believe you — but don't worry about having to cover up your fear. You could even say, "You're really scaring me, but you don't have to do that. I do want to go with you, but . . ." and so on. Some people have escaped rape by claiming they needed to go to the bathroom first, then locking themselves in and crawling out the window or calling for help.

These kinds of tricks can work because the boy wants to believe that you are attracted to him — it's good for his ego. Recent studies of convicted rapists have found that a lot of them rape because they think they are so unattractive to women, they'll never get sex any other way. If you pretend to be willing, you are turning the situation away from an assault into a seemingly normal sexual encounter — until you trick the boy and escape.

Once you have escaped, don't delude yourself into thinking things will be any different on the next date. *Never* go out with him again.

• *If you are assaulted by a date, don't keep it a secret.* This applies even if the assault wasn't successful. Tell your parents or a trusted adult and discuss whether or not to tell a school authority, the boy's family, or the police.

The boy needs to be stopped before he hurts someone else. What is more, you owe it to yourself to get help handling something as traumatic as this; you shouldn't have to do it on your own.

Reporting an assault not only protects yourself and other possible victims, but can help the offender. A boy often molests because he himself is being molested. When the girls in this California junior high decided to tell about a boy who'd been harassing them, students, parents, and faculty alike were grateful.

> Several girls in the school reported that one of the boys was exposing himself to them on the playground. He was also phoning them in the evening and telling them that he was masturbating while he talked to them. The boy was interviewed by Child Assault Prevention counselors and teachers, then a three-hour meeting was held with his parents to help them understand what was going on, why it was happening, and what could be done to help. They were very thankful to be able to intervene before their son moved on to doing worse things, and they were concerned that someone might be abusing him.

PARTIES AND GROUPS

Although staying with groups of people you know is one of the best ways of keeping safe, sometimes groups can get dangerous. Here are some ways to protect yourself:

• *If you're going to a party, try to arrange your transportation home beforehand.* Relying on strangers and acquaintances for rides home is dangerous. Many so-called "date rapes" and "acquaintance rapes" are committed by boys who offer a ride home to a girl they have just met. Call your parents instead, get a taxi, ask a friend to come home and stay with you, or arrange to go home with a friend and stay with her or him.

I'd been at this party till pretty late, and it was time to go. I didn't have a way of getting home without spending a lot of money on a taxi, so this guy I'd just met at the party offered to walk me home. He was a friend of one of my friends, so I said sure. We walked along some dark roads, then he suddenly grabbed me and pulled me into the bushes. He raped me.

• *Don't go to empty houses or wild parties with people you don't know.* Parties are often the scene of gang rapes.

• *If you are with people you don't know, try to avoid getting very drunk or stoned.* You need to keep your wits about you.

• *Whenever you're with a group that includes people you don't know well, avoid going off alone with any one or more of the boys.* This is true at parties, too. Especially avoid going to isolated areas in parks, country lanes, or houses. These are ideal places for rape.

• *If you get high on drugs or drink when you're out, don't go home alone.* This applies day or night. Go home with a friend, take a cab or share one with friends, or call your parents or a trusted friend who drives. You look — and are — especially vulnerable when you are intoxicated, even though you may *feel* stronger, more daring, and safer.

• *If a guy offers to walk you home or give you a ride, ask him where he's going before you tell him your destination, even if you know him well.* If he seems eager to go way out of his way, go with another friend instead. Most people are not willing to travel long distances just to take you home. If they are, you have a right to be suspicious.

• *Don't be embarrassed to turn down rides from a person*

you don't like. If you don't trust him, you feel odd about him in any way, or he has been drinking or taking drugs, turn down the ride. Trust your instincts; very often they prove valid.

• *If you are uneasy in someone's car, sit in the back, make sure the car door unlocks and the seat belt unfastens, and be ready to jump out if you have to.* Although, if you follow the suggestions above, you should never find yourself in this situation.

HOW TO HANDLE GROUP SITUATIONS THAT TURN UGLY

Sometimes parties turn violent or become make-out sessions that can be prime situations for sexual assault. Here's what to do if this happens:

• *If there's any physical violence, leave immediately.* This is true even if the violence doesn't involve you.

• *Act confident and look directly at people.* If there is some kind of cruel teasing going on, you are less likely to be picked on if you don't look scared.

• *Pay attention to your instincts.* If you feel something change in the atmosphere that you don't like — it gets threatening, someone starts insulting someone else, people start ganging up against someone — the sooner you act, the better. Don't hang around hoping things will improve — leave. And get help if the trouble looks serious.

• *If things are really out of hand and you can't run to get help, do something unexpected.* Turn the lights on and off suddenly, turn the music way up or off, break a window, ring the doorbell, shout out that the police are coming. You might save someone from being hurt, assaulted, or raped.

• *If you see that someone at a party is about to get attacked, either sexually or in a fight, don't just stand around doing nothing.* Appeal to a friend to help you stop it, if possible, or leave and call the police from the privacy of another room, from a neighbor's house, or from a street phone. Whether you are a boy whose friends are warming up to a gang assault, or a girl whose friends want to smash up a house, think how bad you'll feel if you go along with them against your will. And don't kid yourself that they won't "really do it." It is always hard to resist the pressure of a group, especially if they are your friends — sometimes it's as if you've forgotten how to think for yourself — but the training you're getting in self-defense in this book should help you fight for your own beliefs. Don't be like this boy:

> When I was in high school, I went to a party once in my hometown. It was late and everyone was high on something. I heard a commotion inside the house and I asked someone what was going on. They said a retarded girl was being gang-banged. I didn't know what to do or how to stop it, so I didn't do anything.

What he should have done was simple enough: gone to the nearest phone and called the police. He didn't even have to identify himself if he didn't want.

JOB INTERVIEWS, NEWSPAPER ROUNDS, SUMMER JOBS

• *If you are going to a job interview at the house of someone you don't know, take a parent or a friend who can wait for you outside.* Sometimes these interviews, especially ones that are advertised in vague terms, are setups for sexual assault.

• *If any job makes you feel uneasy or scared, don't ignore those feelings — figure out why.* Does your employer make you uneasy? Or is it one of the customers? Are you being looked at or treated in a way that is threatening or unpleasant? If you feel in danger, quit.

• *If someone wants you to work in a store by yourself, say no.* Explain that it isn't safe for someone your age, and talk to your employer about ways to make the store safer for everyone, especially in dangerous areas. For example, installing a buzzer system at the door could prevent people from coming in unless you want them to.

• *Let your parents know where your job is and make sure they'll agree to come get you if you ever need help or a ride home.* This precaution isn't designed to curb your independence, it's designed to help you protect yourself. Adults, too, should let people close to them know where they work.

• *Don't take a job delivering newspapers in an area you don't know or don't feel safe in.* If you must, get to know the area and find out from people living there which are the safest streets. Follow the safety rules in the next chapter, *Protecting Yourself Outside.*

HOW TO HANDLE TROUBLE FROM DOCTORS, TEACHERS, AND OTHER PEOPLE IN AUTHORITY

Many people are intimidated by authority figures: employers, parents, doctors, therapists, teachers, coaches; and for young people, almost any adult. It can be hard to stand up to a person in authority if he or she does something wrong to you. You have trouble saying no because you are used to obeying that person. You might be afraid no one would believe you if you told on him or her. Or you might fear that the person will tell embarrassing stories about you, get you into trouble, or take revenge on you. Indeed, molesters usually threaten to do just these things in order to get their victims to comply and to keep quiet. It is important to be able to look up to and admire someone, but when a person abuses his or her power over you by molesting you in any way, that person no longer deserves your respect. Here are some examples of situations like this and what to do about them.

EMPLOYERS

Employers sometimes abuse their power over you with what has come to be known as "sexual harassment." This can mean asking you inappropriately intimate questions about your love life, your body, or your social life, questions like "Do you like sex?" "Do you sleep with your boy/girlfriend?" "Do you have a boy/girlfriend?" "I bet you have lots of guys/girls after you, huh?" "Where did you get that cute bod?" Asking one or two questions may not seem too bad, but if the person persists and won't take your hints that you don't like it, that constitutes sexual harassment.

Sexual harassment can also mean making passes at you, making suggestions that you do something sexual (like posing nude for photographs), or trying to get a date with you. And it can mean actually molesting you, too.

Sarah got a job one summer working as a waitress in a popular café. She needed the money, the place was fun, and she was happy about it. But her boss, a man in his forties with a wife and three kids, wouldn't leave her alone. He flirted with her, touched her all the time, and, worst of all, pinched her behind whenever she walked by him. She didn't say anything because she noticed he did this to the other waitresses too, but it made her summer miserable.

Sarah thought that the other waitresses didn't mind her boss's behavior and was so intimidated by this idea that she didn't stand up for herself. Probably every waitress in the place felt the same way — no one likes to be pinched and bothered all the time. If they had talked among themselves, they could have figured out how to stop their boss. They could have confronted him together and asked him to stop touching them; they could have threatened to strike; or they could have arranged for each one to ask him privately to stop. As a last resort, they could all have walked out on him at once. But even if Sarah couldn't get the other waitresses to cooperate, she could at least have said to him, "Maybe you don't realize this, but you're hurting me and making me miserable by pinching me all the time. Please leave me alone."

A lot of adults and teenagers put up with sexual harassment because they are afraid of losing their job. Like Sarah, you have to decide for yourself how bad you are being made to feel and whether the job is worth it, and also how much danger you might be in. But meanwhile, try these tactics:

1. Tell your boss that you prefer to keep your outside life private.
2. Tell him you'd like to keep the job but want to be left alone. If his approaches have been mild and you are polite but firm, he might get the message and leave you alone.
3. Remember your sexual rights: you have a right not to put up with anyone who makes you feel scared, humiliated, or ashamed. You have a right

to resist and stop any sexual harassment, and you have a right to defy anyone who tries to keep you quiet with threats, promises, or bribes.

Once a boss has sexually molested you or threatened to, you must not only quit the job, you must tell your parents and even the police. What he is doing is illegal, and you have to protect other teenagers who may be less educated in self-defense than you.

DOCTORS

I had a bad cough, so I had to go for a lung X ray. The doctor was an old guy and he was very respected as a lung expert. They made me put on a tiny paper shirt that barely covered me, then when the nurse was out of the room, the doctor made me turn around slowly with my arms in the air. He was looking me up and down in a way I didn't like, so I said, "What are you doing?" and he said, "Looking for your vaccination mark." I said, "You could have asked me, it's on my arm." He just snickered. But I knew he was looking at my breasts.

After that, he made me lie down, and he began to poke and slap and tickle my stomach. Then he started asking me questions about whether I had a boyfriend and if I liked sex and stuff. I got mad and said I didn't answer questions like that. He told me I was rude, and when he took my blood, he stuck the needle in so hard I fainted.

This teenage girl stood up for herself, and because of that, may have stopped any further molestation. But she didn't stop the doctor from taking revenge on her in another way. Several rules got broken here: (1) When a female is being examined by a male doctor, a female nurse is supposed to be in the room at all times. (2) Doctors have power over their patients to make them undress and answer questions, but they are ethically forbidden to take advantage of that in any way. (3) Doctors are certainly not supposed to deliberately hurt patients.

If you ever feel uncomfortable with a doctor, don't be afraid to let him and other people know it.

• *Ask him why he's doing what he's doing.*
• *Ask the nurse to stay with you.*
• *Tell the doctor the instant he hurts you and insist that he stop.*
• *If you think you are being made to take off more clothes than necessary, ask why and say you'd prefer not to.* If you can't see why you have to take off your clothes at all (if the doctor asks you to remove your pants when you've gone in for a chest X ray, for instance), ask for an explanation. If it isn't convincing, refuse.
• *You have a right to have a parent stay with you during the examination, if you want.*
• *If you don't like a doctor, don't be afraid to say so and change doctors.*
• *If a doctor molests you in any way, tell your parents and demand that he be reported to the state health department or the police.* At the least, a doctor who molests can be officially reprimanded. At the most, he can be prosecuted for child sexual abuse and have his license to practice medicine withdrawn.
• *Remember that women doctors can molest, too.* The same rules apply to them.

TEACHERS, COACHES, YOUTH LEADERS

Molesters who take jobs as teachers, athletic coaches, scout leaders, or youth organizers are counting on three things to prevent you from telling on them: your fear of them, your guilt, and your worry that no one would believe you even if you did tell.

They tend to reinforce the first — your fear of them — with threats like these: "I'll flunk you," "I'll tell your parents that you never come to school," "I'll report your behavior to the principal." If you are innocent of these misdeeds, the threats are bad enough — you'll find it hard to convince adults to believe you, a kid, rather than the molester, an adult. But if you have actually broken any rules, these threats are worse. The molester is, in effect, blackmailing you.

Try to always remember that, *whatever you've done, their molesting you is worse.* Any parent or adult who knows anything about sexual assault, or who has read this book, will realize that your misdeeds, if there are any, are nothing compared to what the molester is trying to do to you. They should even praise you for having the guts to tell. Therefore, your answer to the threats of molesters should be, "I don't care. What I've done may be bad, but what you're doing is worse. It's criminal. You can go to jail for it." Then, you should tell a trusted adult what is happening.

Sometimes, the molester will stop at nothing to get you to keep quiet. He'll threaten to kidnap your baby sister, to kill your mother, to wreck your family. In a case like this, it's especially important to get the help of an adult. If no one you know seems suitable — they'll be too shocked or too angry or too scared — go to a rape crisis center or a child abuse agency for help. (See chapter eight, "Getting Help," and "Sources for Safety" for the addresses and phone numbers of places to turn to.)

Molesters prey on the second factor, your guilt, by telling you the assault was your fault. They either say things like "You're such a messed-up kid, you ask for things like that," "You're no good, so you deserve it," and "You really like this, I can tell," or they enlist you in some shameful activity, like looking at or buying pornography, so that you feel too guilty to tell on them. They try to make you feel like a criminal. Again, try to remember that, no matter what you've done, *the assault is never your fault.* You are being manipulated and used, and you have a right to get help.

The third factor that molesters count on, that no one would believe you if you told, can be countered simply by telling. Here are the steps you should take:

• *Start by telling a close friend about the assaults.* This is especially valuable if the molester is someone in your family, like your father or an uncle, or someone the family is close to, like a neighbor or a friend. If you have a friend to help you tell adults, or to go with you to a crisis center, telling can be much easier.

• *Next, ask around among other kids to see if any of them have been molested by this person, too.* If the molester is the father of one of your friends, a teacher, or someone else who has contact with lots of kids, the odds are quite high he is molesting more people than just you. If several kids report him at once, people will be more likely to believe you.

• *After that, tell someone in your family whom you trust.* This is never very easy. Even if the molester is someone the family doesn't know or care about, they will be upset that you've been hurt. But if the molester is someone the family knows and likes, they may be angry, upset, and unwilling to believe you. It's agony for your mother, for instance, to hear that her husband or brother is a child molester. If you don't think you can tell your mother or father about the assaults yet, think of another adult you like instead — a teacher, perhaps; your best friend's mother; an aunt. That adult can help you break the news to your parents. There is more about the difficulties of telling in chapter eight.

• *Finally, if you are sure that you can't tell anyone you know, follow the advice in chapter eight and call a rape crisis or child abuse center.*

OLDER FRIENDS

Sometimes a molester takes advantage of your loneliness (and almost all teenagers go through lonely times) to befriend you, and then to turn that friendship into sex. He might do it by persuading you that sex is a natural part of your relationship. He might do it by threatening to drop you if you don't comply. He might do it by buying you things you normally can't afford so that you feel indebted to him. And because you like him, or even need him, you're afraid to say no.

To avoid even getting into a situation like this, stay away from any older boy (or girl) or any adult who goes out of his way to become your best friend. If you really like the person and don't want to stay away, ask yourself these questions:

1. Are most of his activities centered around people your age?
2. Why is he friends with you instead of someone his age?
3. How much time does he spend with people his own age?

If he does spend most of his time with people his own age, isn't terribly interested in other teenagers but just happens to like you, the friendship is probably okay. If not, he may be a pedophile: he may depend on teens for friendship and for sex. Perhaps he's the kind of pedophile who never actually molests anyone, but don't count on it. Remember that man who spent a year coaching boys on their baseball before he touched them, yet was planning to molest them all along?

If an older friend does try to engage you in any kind of sex, you have a right to resist in any way you need to. Say, "No! I'll tell my mother." "I'll tell the whole team." "I'll tell the whole school." If that doesn't work, you have the right to resist physically. See chapter seven, "Self-Defense," for how to do this. You also have a right and a duty to tell a trusted adult immediately in order to stop the molester from finding another victim. Ask around to see if other teenagers have complaints about him, too, and make sure he is reported to the police. Chapter eight will tell you what to do if you don't want to report him because you are afraid, embarrassed, or you like him too much.

HOW TO HANDLE ASSAULT BY A PARENT

If you are unlucky enough to have a parent who tries to sexually assault you, the only way to protect yourself is to know your sexual rights and refuse to comply. Sometimes verbal and even physical resistance can work, but usually you need outside interference by other adults or the law. A lot of kids try to solve the problem by running away, but that usually only creates other problems. One study of child and teenage prostitutes in San Francisco found that 60 percent of them had run away from sexual assault at home. Now they were being beaten, raped, and otherwise assaulted on the streets.

Being molested by a parent is one of the most devastating traumas possible. The very people who are supposed to protect you from such things are committing them. It makes you feel that your home is a nightmare instead of a haven, that no one loves or ever will love you, and that you can't ever trust anyone in the world.

If you have been sexually assaulted over a long time

by someone in your family, you probably think of yourself as different from anyone else you know. You feel alone, burdened by a shameful secret, and you might look on yourself as somehow dirty and inferior to everyone else. You may also be full of hatred — for the molester, for the rest of the family for not rescuing you, even for yourself. You may, like this teenage victim of incest, try endlessly to find reasons to blame yourself for the assault, as if *you* were the criminal.

I would sit for hours on end and try to think of why this happened to me. I thought of every mistake, every lie, every bad feeling I ever had towards another person. I thought I was being punished for something, but I couldn't think of exactly why.

Try to remember that you are not alone. Hundreds and thousands of children have been sexually abused by their relatives and parents. And try to remember that the assaults didn't happen because of anything you did, who you are, or what you are like. Whether the molester is your father or a stranger, it is *his* hangups, *his* problems, and *his* selfishness that made him abuse you. If you love the person who's been molesting you, it may seem easier to blame yourself for the abuse than to face the fact that he or she is a child molester and a criminal. But blaming yourself makes it harder to recover. And your recovery is more important than his dirty secret.

There are people who will help you. There are solutions to find. But you have to tell someone what is happening. If you keep it a secret, you'll have to live with it in silence for a very long time, and you might not be able to stop it. Keeping it a secret allows your parent to keep doing it to you and maybe to your younger sisters or brothers as well. Keeping it a secret also means your parent will never get the help he needs to stop his behavior.

In chapter seven, "Self-Defense," you will find advice on what to say to stop a parent assaulting you, and what to do physically if you must. In chapter eight, "Getting Help," there is advice on who to tell, how to find help, and what will happen when you do. Never forget that *you deserve all the help you can get.*

FIVE

Protecting Yourself Outside

Self-defense begins with how you look and feel. If you stand and move with confidence, look danger in the eye, and appear alert, you are already frightening off many a potential assailant. This chapter will teach you to look confident, to trust your instincts, and to look after yourself out in the streets. Use it as a sort of recipe for self-protection.

BASIC RULES

TRUST YOUR FEELINGS

The golden rule of self-defense is to pay attention to and trust your instincts. Countless victims of sexual assault and other crimes have said, "I felt something was wrong, but I didn't want to look stupid, so I didn't do anything." If you feel uncomfortable around a person or a place, if a warning signal goes off somewhere deep inside you, if you feel scared or even just uneasy, *don't ignore it.* It is always better to act on your warning instincts and never know whether you were right than to ignore them and find yourself a victim; a moment of looking foolish is nothing compared to being assaulted. Take the story of these two teenage girls:

> We were walking home from school to my house, which was empty, when we heard a man behind us. We both got scared that he was following us, so we did our self-defense yell and ran to a neighbor's house, where we knew someone was home.

Those girls never knew whether they were in danger or not, but by not waiting around to find out, they avoided even taking a risk.

LOOK ALERT

A famous study of muggers, done in the 1970s by a social psychologist named Betty Grayson, has since informed many self-defense groups about how to look "unmuggable." Using a hidden camera, Grayson filmed random pedestrians walking down the street, then showed the film to convicted muggers in prison and asked them to rate the pedestrians for "assaultability." The convicts didn't necessarily pick girls over boys, women over men, or old people over young people, as you might expect. They went for people who looked vulnerable because of the way they walked: they swung their arms out of rhythm with their legs, they plonked their feet down on the pavement with a graceless thump instead of the swinging walk most people have, and they generally looked as if their top halves were separate from their bottom halves. Other observers of muggable types have noticed that they tend to be in a daze, to walk hunched over and with bad posture, to not pay attention to their surroundings, and to look lost. A 1979 census survey found that most crime victims are young men, the group you might expect to be the safest. (Perhaps because young men feel the most invulnerable, they are the least alert on the street.) Anyone out to attack someone on the street is nervous, doesn't want to get caught, and doesn't want to get hurt, so he picks someone who literally looks like a pushover. You can easily avoid looking like that yourself by standing up straight, keeping your feet slightly apart for good balance, and keeping your head up and your mind focused on what's going on around you. You don't have to continually dart worried looks over your shoulder — that only makes you look scared. Just sweep your eyes around once in a while as if you were a politician surveying a crowd. If you look like someone who knows what's going on around you, people will be less likely to pick on you.

DON'T HANDICAP YOURSELF

Part of being alert is avoiding doing and wearing things that make you look especially vulnerable. Radio headsets, for example, make you a walking target because they block out your sense of hearing and hypnotize you with music. Try to avoid getting absorbed in a book, a newspaper, or a map out on the street; don't stand with your head buried in a bag looking for something, or fall asleep in public places. Above all, think about the way you dress. Wobbly or high heels, tight skirts, and any other clothes that hinder your movement are not a good idea if you're planning to walk somewhere — one convicted mugger said he used to hide under stairs and listen for the click-click of high heels, and then he knew he had his victim. Wide-brimmed hats, hoods, sunglasses, umbrellas can obscure your vision and make you more vulnerable, so choose those carefully and be extra alert when you're using them. And loading yourself down with packages or books or a heavy purse is a bad idea, too. If you want to dress up for a party in impractical clothes, but you have to walk or take public transportation, wear sneakers and jeans for the journey and change into the party clothes once you're there. And remember, if you need to carry a purse, don't wind it around your hand or arm — that makes it too easy for someone to pull you over or drag you away to an isolated area.

SAFETY IN THE STREET

- *When you leave home, carry your keys separately from your purse, wallet, I.D., and address.* That way, if you lose your keys or something with your address on it, you won't risk giving a criminal access to your house.
- *When you're out, always have enough money for a phone call.* Money for a bus or cab is a good idea, too. Some people who live in high-crime areas always make sure they carry some money in case they are mugged — muggers occasionally get so infuriated if you have nothing that they'll hurt you out of anger.
- *Know where you are going.* If you are somewhere unfamiliar, figure out your route before you leave so that you won't get or look lost.
- *Don't take shortcuts* through parking lots, alleyways, or other isolated areas, especially if you are alone.
- *Avoid vacant buildings*, empty lots, and sparsely populated streets.
- *If you are in an unfamiliar place, pay extra attention to your gut feelings.*
- *Don't wait in a car alone in a parking lot or garage.* If you do find yourself in a car alone and you feel at all uneasy, lock the doors and roll the windows up most of the way. If anyone you don't know approaches, don't unlock the doors or roll the windows down.
- *If you go to the same place every day — to and from school, for instance — try to vary the route you take.* Choose differ-

ent streets once in a while, or meet a friend on the way there or back for a change. This can foil anyone who might have been watching you.

• *If you live in a city, be aware of which streets have doormen, open stores, and good lighting.* If you live in the suburbs or in a small town, know which streets have houses where people are usually at home, and which ones have plenty of streetlights. That way, you'll know where to go should you ever feel scared or need help.

• *If you jog, try not to go alone.* Choose a busy area and time of day, keep aware of your surroundings, avoid shrubbery and isolated areas, don't use an earphone radio, and keep the last part of the run, when you are most tired, for the safest place.

• *If you see a group of men or boys on the street, don't walk through them.* Cross the street, go around them, or even double back and choose another block.

• *If you are passing a possible source of danger, like a couple of guys lurking on a corner or in a dark entranceway, look at it.* Don't pretend to yourself that it'll go away if you don't. When you know what's around you, it's harder for someone to take you by surprise.

• *When getting into a car, alone or with someone else, check the back seat first.* Assailants sometimes hide there.

• *You are no safer on bicycle than on foot.* Don't bike where you wouldn't walk, and follow the safety rules above.

HOW TO HANDLE HARASSMENT, FLASHERS, AND OTHER ASSAULTS

IF YOU ARE HARASSED ON THE STREET

Most of the time, the men who shout at you in the street don't mean you any physical harm. But once in a while, they may test you to see how likely a victim you might make for an assault, or they may be spoiling for a fight. You'll have to judge the situation for yourself. If you feel at all afraid, or you are in a deserted place, pretend you didn't hear the remarks, don't talk back, and don't get physically close to the harasser. Walk away briskly with your head held high, looking confident and unworried. If you feel humiliated, pretend that you are deaf and really didn't hear him, or fantasize that you have magic powers that will make him crumple up in pain. Picture yourself pounding the guy into the pavement, if you want, or saying to him what he said to you. And remember, anyone who gets a kick out of shouting at women in the street is proving himself a coward. By not responding to him, you are being dignified, not afraid.

If you feel safe enough, you could respond by saying something like "You have no right to speak to me like that," calmly and flatly. It's better not to shout obscenities or get into a verbal fight — that will only prolong the unpleasantness and might, in rare circumstances, provoke physical violence. If you can answer calmly and with conviction, you may, like this girl below, have the satisfaction of refusing to be a passive victim to this kind of everyday assault.

I was walking down the street feeling happy, when two workmen began shouting obscene things at me. Their intrusion on my mood and my privacy made me furious. So I stopped and shouted at them, "I have as much right to walk down the street without getting hassled as you do! Leave me alone!" They stood there for several seconds with their mouths hanging open before they remembered to be cool and laugh. I was embarrassed afterwards, but I felt satisfied, too.

IF YOU SEE A FLASHER

Pretending not to see an exhibitionist is the safest reaction, even though it can be frustrating — you'd probably rather find some way to humiliate him or frighten him back. Get away from him as fast as possible, and if he's hanging around other kids, report him to a teacher, your parents, or anyone else suitable. If you know where he tends to hang out, telling the police is a good idea, too. He might not be that hard to catch.

IF YOU ARE BEING FOLLOWED ON FOOT OR BY CAR

I was walking up the hill to visit a friend when I noticed this boy crouching on the sidewalk in front of me, tying his shoelaces. He was about fourteen. At first I didn't think anything of it, then I noticed he was exposing himself! He kept following me up the hill, letting me walk ahead of him, then running around in front of me and exposing himself again. I looked around for some way of getting away from him, but on one side were small, deserted streets and a huge, multi-level car park, which I knew wasn't safe. On the other side was the college campus, which was full of trees and bushes and was empty 'cause it was Sunday. I kept walking and crossing the street, whistling and humming so he'd think I didn't see him, but he kept following me and I got scared. I also felt stupid, being afraid of a young boy like that, but I didn't know if he was crazy or might turn violent if I spoke to him. So I kept walking.

In the end, I got to a store and went in and called the police. I didn't want to lead the guy to my friend's house because I knew she was alone. The whole time I was on the phone, I saw him hiding behind a tree, waiting for me, but by the time the police got there, he was gone.

Most of the things this girl did to safeguard herself were sensible: she knew not to go off somewhere even more isolated, which would have been more dangerous, and she knew not to let this exhibitionist know where she was going. But she forgot one possibility; she could have turned and gone back in the direction she came from, toward a busier street.

If you think you're being followed, don't dismiss your fear as paranoia — act. Turn around and look. Cross the street. On a main street, stop and look in a store window, using it as a mirror to watch the person you suspect. If he persists in following you, run into a store or a neighbor's house and call a parent or friend to come and get you. If, like the girl above, you can't find anywhere safe to run to, return the way you came, making sure you don't pass within grabbing distance of the follower. If you are really scared, go to the nearest house that has people at home and ask them to call your parents and the police. Another solution, and a simple one if you are in a busy area, was found by this fourteen-year-old boy:

> I was walking home with a big pizza pie one night when some guys shouted, "Hey, come over here!" I didn't like the look of them, so I shouted back, "I can't, I've got to deliver this pizza." They crossed the street and started coming at me, so I went in a store and asked two women in there if they'd walk me home. They did, and I was okay.

There's never any point in risking your safety out of pride or the fear of looking foolish. Never be afraid to ask for help.

If you notice a car following you along the curb and you are in a city or town, run across the street and toward a busy, populated area as quickly as possible. If you are on a deserted country road, get off the road and run to a house, or hide somewhere you know no one could find you, like up a tree. Don't go deep into woods or fields unless you know a secret way home that no one else could find. *Never lead anyone who is following you to your home.*

IF YOU ARE MUGGED

Most muggers only want your money. Most of them are also scared. That's why you should *never* fight any mugger who has a weapon, who has friends with him, who can clearly overpower you, or who seems liable to panic and hurt you in any way. Your physical safety is never worth a wallet or a watch. Some muggers, however, are also potential rapists, and that's also why you should never antagonize one — he might get mad and decide to punish you with a sexual attack. If you are mugged, keep calm by taking steady breaths, tell the guy exactly what valuables you have on you and where they are (don't try to hide anything because if he finds it, he might get angry and hurt you), and offer to hand them over to him. If he says okay, move slowly, telling him exactly what you are doing: "I am taking my wallet out of my pocket. I am taking my watch off to give you." Further hints: look at his face, not at the weapon — it makes you seem calmer, which will help him not to panic (unless, of course, he expressly tells you not to look at him). Remember, he is scared, too — if you can keep calm, you can help to calm him. Don't act contemptuous, don't beg or plead, and don't provoke him.

If a mugger tries to make you go somewhere more

isolated with him, like a car or a parking lot, or if he tries to force you into your home, you have a more dangerous situation on your hands. See chapter seven, "Self-Defense," for ways to prevent this.

IF YOU ARE JOSTLED OR OTHERWISE BOTHERED

There are several set ways in which assailants of all kinds try to test out potential victims on the street: they bump into you and shove you, they purposely block your way, they walk right up to you, or stand unnaturally close to you in a crowd, they look you up and down and appear to enjoy your discomfort, or they start talking to you as if they know you really well. If any of these things happen, don't just ignore or put up with it, move away quickly and walk off without showing fear or shock. Look firm but not frightened, as if you're thinking, *I know what you're up to, but you're not going to bother me.* Make your face as expressionless as possible, and don't make any comment. This way you will look alert, dignified, and tough; not like the passive, easily scared person they are seeking. If you don't think you can cover up your fear with a stony face, practice in the mirror.

You might also find yourself being threatened in some way by someone you are truly not scared of. If so, you may be able to have the kind of satisfaction this girl got when she spoke up for herself.

I was walking home from the train station in my town, when I noticed that a boy had been following me ever since I got off the train. He was fat and slow and real young-looking and I just wasn't scared of him, so I turned around suddenly — he was right there behind me and already panting with the effort of keeping up with me — and I said, "Stop following me. You should be ashamed of yourself." He got all embarrassed and left.

IF SOMEONE OFFERS OR ASKS FOR HELP

If a stranger offers to help you carry packages or to give you a ride, stand tall and confident and say, "No thank you." Then walk briskly away. If you've followed the "Don't handicap yourself" rule listed under "Basic Rules," you'll never be loaded-down enough to need help.

A common trick that both muggers and rapists use is to work in pairs: one person intimidates you on the street, the other one pretends he's a kind stranger and offers to walk you somewhere safe. The pair can be two men or a man and a woman. If this happens, say no firmly and get away fast. If the "helper" persists, run into a store and get help, or do the self-defense yell (described in chapter seven) and run.

If someone asks you directions, don't go too close to him, especially if he's in a car, for he could snatch you and drag you inside. Either say "I don't know" and keep walking if the person seems unpleasant, or shout your directions from a distance as if you are in a hurry to get someplace.

A man once beckoned me over to his car, waving a map as if he was lost. I went over and looked in. He was masturbating.

If the people asking directions are a family, or tourists in obvious need of help, there's probably no need to be suspicious. But be wary of lone men, men in groups, and even couples.

If a man or woman comes up to you on the street and asks for help, or you see someone lying down and groaning, there are ways to help without putting yourself in unnecessary danger. Offer to phone the police or an ambulance from the nearest phone booth but don't get too close to the person and don't accompany him to an isolated area; it could be a trick. You'll have to use your own judgment on this, of course, because if you think someone's really hurt, you may choose to risk being tricked in order to help. There are always times when being a "good citizen" entails some personal risk. If the person refuses your offer to call for help, however, he or she may not be as badly off as you think.

IF ANYONE BOTHERS YOU WHILE YOU ARE JOGGING

If someone jostles you, shouts at you, runs too close to you, or follows you while you are running, change direction if you can and run quickly toward a populated area. Go into a store, if possible, or stop someone else and tell him or her what's happening.

IF YOU HAVE TO TURN TO A STRANGER FOR HELP

Once, when I was being followed, I stopped a young man on the street and told him what was happening. I asked him to walk with me for a block as if he knew me, in the hope it would frighten the creep off. The man said, "I don't have time. Why don't you cut through that parking lot?" Not only was I shocked at his unwillingness to help even though I was in danger, but I realized he'd made a suggestion that would have put me in even more danger.

Unfortunately, relying on strangers for help has its risks, too. They might not be willing to help at all, they might make dangerous suggestions, or they might even take advantage of your vulnerability and attack you themselves. You should take these precautions: If you go into a store for help or to use the phone, stay in the public area. Don't go into a back room or a basement with someone you don't know. Insist on calling your parents or the police, rather than taking a ride from a stranger. Don't take suggestions that are contrary to the advice in this book.

SAFETY AT NIGHT

- *Try to avoid walking alone at night anywhere.*
- *Share a taxi home with friends* rather than walking or taking public transportation.
- *Keep enough money on you* so that you never get stuck somewhere without the fare home.
- *Try to get your parents to agree to pick you up,* no questions asked, if it's late and you can't get home safely.
- *Try to walk on streets you know,* especially those with people you know at home and with open stores.
- *Always choose a busy street over a quiet one,* even if it means a longer walk.
- *Walk on the outside of the curb.* Stay away from entrances to houses and alleyways.
- *If you feel nervous, walk in the road facing traffic instead of on the sidewalk.* Make sure you are wearing or carrying something white so cars can see you.
- *If someone is walking toward you and you feel nervous, cross the street.* Look up at the nearest lit window and wave as if you're being watched.
- *If you need help from a neighbor or the nearest house and you can't rouse the people, don't hesitate to make a huge ruckus.* If all else fails, throw a stone through a window. You'll probably scare the assailant off, if nothing else.

• *All these precautions apply even if you are walking with friends.* A friend or two isn't always protection, especially late at night.

SAFETY IN PUBLIC PLACES

If you like to hang out in parks, at the beach, in video arcades, pizza parlors, shopping malls, or any other open, public place, take these precautions:

• *Stay with your friends,* or at least within sight of them.

• *Avoid these places at night,* especially if they tend to be deserted or to attract gangs.

• *If you are getting stoned or drunk with friends, stick together for protection.* You are more vulnerable in that condition, and if you wander off alone, you won't be as alert and streetwise as you should be.

• *Avoid deserted restrooms.* Go with a friend.

• *Keep an eye out for lone adults,* especially men or older boys, who hang out in places like malls, arcades, and anywhere else kids congregate. If you notice a lone man hovering around trying to make friends with you, your friends, or younger kids, ask yourself why he isn't with people his own age. If he tries to make friends with you, or he offers you money, food, drink, or drugs, refuse and act cold and distant. If he persists, or you see him playing a lot with a particular kid, tell the staff of the arcade, your parents, or another trusted adult about him: he may well be a molester. If you notice that he especially likes to befriend kids or teenagers who are unpopular or lonely, be particularly suspicious. You could try to warn the kids, too, or even call their parents if you know them. You can protect yourself and your friends now with your new knowledge about self-defense.

• *If you want to go on a long walk in the park or in the*

country by yourself, think about how safe you'll feel and what you could do should anyone try to attack you. How near would you be to houses or streets where you could get help? Are there ranger stations in the park, and do you know where they are? Do you know your way out of the park, or your way home? Being alone in the woods, on a beach, or in the country can be a romantic, dreamy experience and no amount of self-defense awareness should make you feel that you can't take that walk. You have as much right to enjoy nature as anyone else. But at the same time, you should be cautious. If your local park is known to be unsafe at certain hours, don't go in at those times. If you are on vacation near a state park with wonderful hiking trails, make sure someone knows where you are going and when you expect to be back, then go ahead. If you are in an area where there's one crime a year, take what precautions you can, relax, and enjoy yourself. You can't worry all the time.

SAFETY WHILE TRAVELING

Whether you are going on a special vacation or just taking the bus to school, here are some safety tips you should know and follow:

• *Stay alert while waiting for a bus or train.* Be aware of what is going on around you, stand in a balanced position, and, if you are in a dangerous area, stand with your back to the wall so you can't be approached from behind. Never stand on the edge of a train platform or within reach of a passing train: someone could grab your necklace or shoulder bag and drag you along the platform.

• *Avoid isolated bus stops and train stations,* if possible, especially in cities and at night.

• *Get your money ready in your hand* so that you don't

have to fumble around with your head buried in a wallet or purse.

• *Sit near the driver or conductor* if the train or bus is empty, or if there are suspicious-looking people around you.

• *If you're on vacation in a place you don't know well, ask people you know which areas to avoid and which streets are the busiest and safest.* Study the map before you go out — *not* on the street — and learn your way around so that you don't look lost and bewildered.

• *Don't hitchhike.* Convicted rapists have told interviewers that they see hitchhikers as ready-made victims and even go cruising for them when they want to rape. Boys are often victimized this way because they think it's safe for them to hitchhike. Hitching is so dangerous, whether you're with a friend or on your own, that the adventure of it simply isn't worth the risk.

If you absolutely must hitch, here are some essential precautions: Trust your instincts and never get into a car with anyone who makes you feel funny in any way. Don't get into a car that has more than one man in it. Ask the driver where he or she is going before you state your destination, and if they say they'll go out of their way for you, don't get in — most normal people wouldn't go way out of their way just to get you home. Sit in the back. Make sure the door is unlocked. Keep your luggage with you at all times. *Before* you get in, look for door handles — if there aren't any, don't get in. If you are with a friend, don't let yourselves get separated into the front and back seats. If you are a boy hitching with a girlfriend, she should get in last and get out first. Don't take rides with people who are drunk or stoned. And don't think that if you are in another country you are automatically safe.

Even if you take all these precautions, you are still at

risk. Couples rape, businessmen rape, grandfathers rape. When you are making yourself as vulnerable as you are when you hitch, you can't trust anyone.

HOW TO HANDLE TROUBLE WHILE TRAVELING

IF SOMEONE MOLESTS YOU

I was on the subway in rush hour, and a man started putting his hand up my skirt. I was so shocked that I couldn't do anything, but just stood there while his hand crept higher and higher. I kept wondering, "Can anyone see? Do they think I like this?" and hoping someone would help me. Ever since, I've felt ashamed every time I think of it, 'cause I just stood there doing nothing.

A lot of people react to being molested like that — they freeze. Afterward, they hate themselves for it. Freezing is a shocked reaction to something unexpected; now that you know it can happen to you, you'll probably be able to unfreeze pretty quickly. If anyone rubs up against you, feels you up, or exposes himself to you on a bus or train, move away immediately. Go to the driver or conductor and complain. If there are people around you, shout "This man is bothering me!" or "There's a pervert in here!" and get away from him. Make sure the guy doesn't follow you off the bus or train and if he does, take the suggestions below.

IF YOU ARE BEING WATCHED OR FOLLOWED

If you catch someone staring at you, look directly at him for a second. Don't stare or engage in any prolonged eye contact, but just let him know you've seen him. If anyone who's been bothering you looks as if he's about to follow you off the bus or train, step back and let him get off first, then stay on to the next stop. If he doesn't get off, stay on until you get to a stop near stores and a phone, so you can call your parents and ask them to come and get you.

Whenever you are being followed, don't go straight home. Go to a store, or a friend or neighbor's house (if possible), and call for help. And *always* stay in a populated area.

IF SOMEONE TALKS TO YOU PERSISTENTLY

I was stuck on a train once during a breakdown, and this middle-aged man started chatting to me. I didn't like him 'cause he was pushy, so I acted cold and moved away from him. He got the message, but then he turned to this young teenage girl and started talking to her. She was too embarrassed to be rude to him, and pretty soon he was touching her earrings and necklace and asking about her boyfriends and making her blush. She looked extremely embarrassed, 'cause everyone could hear.

Don't let someone intimidate you into putting up with pushy, personal, or unpleasant conversation. That may be all this type of molester (and it is a kind of molesting to force intimacy on a stranger) wants, but he may be testing to see how compliant a victim you might be. If he's insensitive enough to keep bothering you, you don't have to worry about being rude to him. If brief, cold answers and a turned-away head don't stop him, pointedly moving away from him should. If you are absolutely stuck next to him in a rush-hour crowd, say, "I don't answer questions like that" or shout, "There's a man bothering me here, please let me through." Make sure *he's* the one who is embarrassed, not you.

SAFETY COMING HOME

Coming into your home, especially in an apartment building, is one of the most dangerous moments of your day. Muggers and rapists often choose to hide and ambush people in lobbies, hallways, and doorways because they are hidden from the street. Here are some precautions to take:

• *If you live in an apartment building, arrange a safety code ring with your family.* If, for example, you are stuck downstairs with someone you are afraid of, you could pretend to be visiting the building and ring your apartment bell in the prearranged code. That way, anyone at home will know to call the police and come down to help you.

• *If there is a hidden nook in your building — behind the elevator or by the mailboxes in an apartment building, behind bushes or a garage in a house — talk to your parents about it.* They should get the landlord to either block off the area with a wall or put up a mirror to reflect anyone hiding there. If you live in a house, your parents should cut back bushes that could hide assailants, block off hideaway entrances, and install safety lighting.

• *Always have your keys in your hand before you approach your front door.* Fumbling for keys in a hidden doorway makes it easy for an offender to attack you or force you in with him.

• *If someone suspicious is hanging around your entrance-way, don't go in.* Walk past. Wait. Phone home from a phone booth if someone is there who could come to get you. Go to a local store or a neighborhood friend for help.

• *As you enter the lobby of an apartment building, look behind you quickly, and look in the mirrors to make sure no one is hiding around a corner.* Shut the door quickly behind you. If you see anyone, get back out of the building as soon as possible and go to a phone to call for help.

• *A person who enters your apartment building with a key in his hand doesn't necessarily live there.* If you've never seen that person before, let him go in first — if he can't unlock the door or he tries to make you unlock it for him, pretend you've forgotten something and leave.

• *Don't let anyone into your building or house you don't know.* This is difficult when you want to be polite and a good neighbor, but too many offenders gain access to homes this way. Either pretend you don't see the person if he or she comes up behind you as you enter, and close the door quickly behind you, or ask them to please ring the bell of the person they are visiting. You could say, "I'm sorry, but it's building policy not to let people we don't know in. Please buzz the people you are visiting." If the person insists, be firm or just end the conversation by walking away and leaving him outside the locked door. Any decent visitor would respect your caution.

• *Anytime you don't like the look of someone entering the building with you, maybe only because you've never seen him before, go back out and call home.*

• *If you find your door open or unlocked when you get home and it shouldn't be,* don't go in. You don't want to surprise thieves in the act; they may turn violent. Instead, go to a neighbor's, call the police, and call your parents, then wait for the police to arrive and let them go in before you. *Never confront a burglar.* A scared burglar is a dangerous burglar.

• *If you come home alone and feel scared for any reason, stand by the door and yell something like "I'm home!"* and wait until you hear a response. If no one in your family answers, or if you still feel scared, don't go in. Go to a friend's instead, or ask a neighbor you know well to go in with you. Sometimes people subconsciously sense that an intruder is in their home: perhaps the place smells different, or some everyday object is out of place or missing. If you habitually feel scared coming home alone, talk to your parents about what can be done to make you feel safer. A good family practice is for anyone coming in to yell, "Mom's home," or whoever it is, to let anyone else home know who's there.

All these precautions may seem paranoid and a little overwhelming, but with practice they'll soon become second nature. Take a refresher course once in a while and look this chapter over again — it's a lot to remember all at once. All these ways of protecting yourself are so logical and simple that they will soon sink in. And they will go a long way toward preventing you from ever getting assaulted.

SIX

Protecting Yourself Inside

Almost a third of all sexual attacks occur inside or near the victim's home, just where we all feel the safest. Many others happen in other places we normally consider safe, too, like school or a friend's house. Here are some ways to keep yourself safer inside.

SAFETY AT HOME ALONE

If you don't feel safe when you are at home alone, talk to your parents about what can be done to make your home safer. If they say, "Don't be silly" or "Don't be a scaredycat," point out that 44 percent of burglars walk into houses through unlocked doors and windows, and that many of those burglars, given the opportunity, turn into rapists. Then ask your parents these questions:

• *What locks are on the doors?* Does your family use them? A lock is no good unless it's used. All outside doors should have a deadbolt lock at least an inch long, and all windows should lock, too. Most local police departments will survey the safety of your house or apartment for free, and suggest what is needed.

• *Is there a window that might be easy to break through?* You could put a few potted plants and vases in front of it so that anyone breaking in would make a terrible clatter.

• *Are there hidden keys in the garage, under the doormat, or under a flowerpot?* Hidden keys are an invitation to intruders. Tell your parents to trust you and your siblings with your own set of keys instead.

• *Who else has the keys to your home, and how much do you trust those people?* There have been several cases of burglaries and rapes committed by building superintendents or their sons. Discuss this with your family and consider changing the locks.

• *Is the garage locked?* An open garage gives intruders easy access to tools and a ladder, as well as providing them with a convenient hiding place while they break in. You might as well give them a key.

• *Do you know your neighbors, and can they see if someone is breaking into your home?* Suggest a policy of watching each other's house or apartment. Get rid of shrubbery that hides windows and doors. Entrances should be well lit at night.

When you are at home alone, there are many ways in which you can make yourself safer. Home should be a safe haven, but you have to make it so yourself.

• *Have a family imagination session.* You can all pretend you are burglars trying to break into your home. Where are the vulnerable spots (cellar, back door, kitchen window?) and what can you do to safeguard them?

• *Make a family Safe Room.* This is a room, closet, or bathroom that has a telephone extension and a good lock on the inside. If burglars break into your home and you cannot get out, your family can retreat to the Safe Room, lock themselves in, and call the police. With luck, you can do this before the intruders even know you are there.

• *Paste 911 and your local police number on the phone* in case your mind blanks out in an emergency.

• *Leave a few lights on around the house* so you don't look as if you're by yourself.

• *Always close curtains and blinds at night.* That way, people won't be able to watch you.

• *Lock the doors behind you when you are inside.*

• *Avoid going to deserted areas of the building alone.* This includes the basement, laundry room, and roof.

• *If you live in an apartment building, never buzz in anyone you don't know or expect.* Always use the intercom to ask who it is, and be sure you recognize the voice. If someone says, "It's me," ask, "Who's me?" If there is no intercom, arrange a code ring with friends so that you know it's not a stranger at the door. Choose an unlikely ring, like four short buzzes and a long one. Everyone uses two rings.

• *Don't open the door to anyone you don't know.* Always use the peephole to make sure you recognize the person.

If you are home alone and someone knocks or rings at the door, follow these steps:

1. *Ask who it is through the door.* If it's someone you don't know, call out, "I've got it, Dad," so that you don't seem to be alone.
2. *Look through the peephole.* Never rely on the doorchain — someone could easily stick a weapon through or break open the door.
3. *If you don't know or trust the person, ask him or her to slip a business card under the door and to come back later.* You could say, "My parents are busy right now, please leave a message."
4. *If it's a delivery, ask the person to leave it on the*

doorstep. If he has a paper for you to sign, tell him to slip it under the door. Anyone genuine will respect your caution.

5. *If it's a repairperson you don't expect, ask to see a business card and call the company to make sure they really sent the person to your house.* If the person at your door is a con artist, he'll probably go away as soon as he realizes you are checking on him.

6. *If it's a repairperson you do expect, ask him or her to slip a business card under the door.* A lot of assailants, including the Boston Strangler, have gotten into homes by posing as repairmen. Some of them even have uniforms.

7. *Never give your address to anyone you don't know, in person or on the phone.* The exception to this, of course, is when you have to call the police, fire department, or an ambulance service in an emergency.

8. *NEVER LET ON THAT YOU ARE ALONE.*

HOW TO HANDLE ATTEMPTED AND ACTUAL BREAK-INS

• *If someone at your door won't go away even when you use the precautions described above, phone your neighbors and the police immediately.* This applies if the person gets threatening or acts persistent, stubborn, or suspicious in any way. Make sure your doors and windows are locked, too.

• *If you hear someone break into the house, remember—DON'T CONFRONT A BURGLAR.* Try to get out by another exit immediately, run to a neighbor, and call the police. If you can't get out, retreat to the Safe Room, lock it, and quickly and quietly call the police, giving them your address first.

• *If you see a strange car parked in front of your house and any evidence that there's been a break-in, DON'T GO IN.* Take the license number, go to a neighbor's, and call the police.

• *If you see a Peeping Tom (someone who watches you through a window or door, hoping you won't see him), lock your doors and windows immediately and call the police.* Call a neighbor, too, and ask him to come over. Some Peeping Toms are hoping to do more to you than just peep.

CONS TO KNOW ABOUT

Criminals are very resourceful about thinking of ways to get into your house. Here are some you should recognize:

• *A woman comes to the door with a big bunch of flowers and says they are a surprise gift for your mother.* In one city, this trick was used to get a burglary team into homes. Tell her to leave the flowers on the doorstep and then don't open the door until she has left.

• *A man, woman, or child comes to your door pleading for help.* "My wife's having a baby. I've got to get her to the hospital. Can I use your phone?" is a common one. "My car's broken down. Can I use your phone?" is another. "I need to use your bathroom." "My mother is hurt." Even — sadly — "I've just been raped, please let me in." Kids and women are sometimes part of con games. By all means offer to help, but do it, if at all possible, without opening your door. Offer to call the police or an ambulance and quickly take the details of their needs. Push some money under the door, if you feel you should. Call a neighbor to come over to help. Only in obviously desperate cases — if a person is bleeding or visibly hurt — should you open the door.

• *Someone falls with a thud against your door.* Call the

police and a neighbor. Don't open the door until they arrive.

• *Someone tells you he's arrived for an emergency repair, like a dangerous gas leak in your house.* Ask for the name of his company, his business identification, and phone to check first.

• *A man, woman, or couple arrive and say they are old friends of your parents dropping in for a surprise visit.* Say through the door: "My parents cannot be disturbed now. Could you leave a name or number?"

• *Someone at the door claims they are doing a survey.* Don't open the door. Say, "Please slip the necessary papers under the door. I don't open the door to strangers."

HOW TO HANDLE SUSPICIOUS OR OBSCENE PHONE CALLS

• *If you get an obscene, silent, or heavy-breathing call, hang up immediately but calmly.* Don't slam the phone down in a fluster and don't say anything. If the surprise has made you gasp or shout, don't feel bad about it but be prepared for the caller to try again. If he does, either get your father or a brother with a grown-up voice to answer a few times, or don't answer the phone at all. If the caller persists over several days, tap the phone with a pen, as if the call is being traced, or cup your hand lightly over the mouthpiece and whisper, "This is him, officer." Only try this last trick if you can sound convincing. Also, try not to talk about the calls to friends and acquaintances — obscene callers are often people who know you, and to hear that you are distressed is just what they need to keep wanting to bother you. Finally, if the caller won't give up, call the police and the phone company for further advice and help. You may have to change your phone number.

• *If someone calls up and says, "Guess who this is," don't.* Say, "I don't play guessing games on the phone. Say who you are or I'll hang up," and hang up immediately if the person won't identify himself. If it is a friend, explain that guessing games are a common con that criminals use to exploit potential victims. They often turn obscene.

• *If someone calls up and says, "Who is this?" or "Is this . . ." and lists your number, don't give him the answer he wants.* Say, "Who's calling, please?" and "Who are you trying to reach?" Make him identify himself before saying who you are. Criminals often try to find out where you live with these tricks.

• *If a person you don't know calls and asks to speak to your parents, don't let on that you are home alone.* Say, "My mother's in the shower/in the garden/taking a nap/busy; can I take a message?" Then get hold of your parents if you can and pass the message on. If the caller insists on trying to get more information out of you, stick to whatever you told him and sound firm — no "ums" and "ahs" or "I guess's." You don't want to show that you are lying or he'll guess you are alone.

• *Never give anyone you don't know well personal information on the phone.* A common ruse of burglars and other criminals is to pose as school district survey takers, or some kind of market research firm. Before you know it, you are being asked about your daily habits, where you live, and your sex life. No real survey about sexuality would ask you questions on the phone at all.

• *If you are home alone, and a caller scares you in any way by saying something like "I know where you live and I'm coming to get you," or "I can see you right now," hang up and call your neighbor and the police.* You may not be in any real danger, but there's no point in waiting around to find out.

SAFETY IN ELEVATORS

Offenders often trap people in the elevators of apartment buildings, public buildings, and offices. This enables them to either stop the elevator between floors, so they can assault you where you can't escape, or to force you to a roof or basement, which puts you in even more danger. Take these precautions:

• *When in doubt, use the stairs.* Running up and down stairs, where you have a chance of getting away or knocking at a door for help, is much safer than being trapped in an elevator.

• *Never get into an elevator with anyone who makes you uneasy.* Pretend you've forgotten something and say, "Go ahead," then use the stairs or wait for the next elevator.

• *When you get on, check the buttons to see where the elevator is going.* If you can tell that it's headed for the basement, get off. Basements are dangerous.

• *Once you are on, stand near the controls and face the door.* Look at the people coming in, not up at the numbers or down at the floor. This makes you look more alert and confident.

• *If anyone makes you uneasy or bothers you, press all the buttons to make the elevator stop as soon as possible, get out at the nearest floor, and run to the most populated area of the building.* Call for help if you need to. Leave the building if you can.

SAFETY IN SCHOOL

Schools, especially large ones, can be dangerous places. Hallways and bathrooms are often deserted; locker rooms, gyms, and basements can be hidden and far away from populated areas. Here are some safety measures:

• *Avoid deserted places in school.* This is especially true if you are alone, out during a class period, or staying late.

• *If you see a suspicious-looking person hanging around the school, like a man who doesn't have any connection to the place, report him to a trusted teacher immediately.* Child molesters are often attracted to schools. If he turns out to be legitimate, don't worry about feeling like a fool; you've been alert and cautious and everyone should respect that.

• *If you know of anyone in the school molesting a student, report it.* You aren't being a tattletale, you are having the courage to bring to light a crime that many people are too afraid to face. Cases of teachers or school janitors molesting hundreds of kids without being caught are fairly common: they can rely on their victims being too ashamed and afraid to tell.

• *If you are bothered by anyone in the school, you have a right to stop him or her.* This is true whether the person is a teacher, a friend, or even the principal. Being bothered can mean being touched, teased, tickled, or wrestled repeatedly against your will; receiving obscene phone calls; being threatened or bullied; or actually being sexually molested. The ways to stop these behaviors range from saying, "Stop bothering me. You have no right to do it and I don't like it," to telling an adult about the incidents, to physically fighting back. A self-defense teacher in California told of how a fourteen-year-old girl handled persistent harassment by a fellow student:

A boy at school, who was somewhere between twelve and fourteen, liked this girl, but the only way he could show it was to pinch and poke her all the time. She couldn't even get a drink at the water fountain in the schoolyard without this boy bothering her, and she couldn't stand it. She told him twice to stop it, but he just said, "Oh yeah, big tough you. What are you going to do about it?" When he did it the third time, she said, "One more time and I'll hurt you." He did it again, so she whirled around and did her self-defense kick into his knee. His knee was hurt — not permanently, but enough to stop him [from] bothering her. She became a heroine at school because this boy had been bothering a lot of people. Even the boy's parents were supportive because they didn't like the way their son treated girls.

A physical defense like this should only be the last resort, but if someone is hurting you, you have a right to do whatever you have to to stop it.

• *If relations between the sexes at your school involve a lot of bullying and hostility, try to get your school to bring in an educational program about sexual assault.* In various locations around the country, there are organizations that specialize in visiting schools to teach teenagers and teachers about sexual assault — what causes it and what to do about it. Many of them give workshops designed to help boys and girls talk to each other about the problems they are having getting along. Programs like this are listed in the back of this book. Sometimes even one visit by a program can work wonders, as it did in this California junior high:

The seventh- and eighth-grades were brought together for a discussion by the CAP [Child Assault Prevention] Training Center teacher. The girls said to the boys, "All through elementary school you were our friends. Now you're acting like enemies — flipping our skirts, making nasty comments to us, grabbing our bodies. That's a violation of our privacy. It's not fair. Why are you doing that?"

The boys had several responses: "I thought you liked that . . ." "I don't know how else to get a

girl's attention . . ." "Somebody dared me to do it
. . ." "I used to flip the girls' skirts, then a couple
of friends said it wasn't cool, so I stopped." Finally
a boy said, "Okay, we'll change, but the girls have
to acknowledge us when we change." Another boy
said, "I'm afraid to go talk to a girl just as a friend,
because then everyone is going to think there's
something going on between us and start teasing
me, and I hate that."

After that, the teacher got the girls and boys to
draw up a list of ten things they could each do to
improve communication between them and to cut
down on abusive remarks and actions.

SAFETY WHILE BABYSITTING

As harmless as babysitting seems, it does, unfortunately, make you somewhat vulnerable. You are alone
in a house you may not be familiar with; you are working for people you may not know well; you have the
responsibility of looking after the safety of young children as well as your own; and you often have to go
home late. Many of the rules listed under "Safety at
Home Alone" at the beginning of this chapter apply to
babysitting, too, but here are some additions:

• *Meet your employers before you start.* If you feel uncomfortable about either of them, don't take the job.

• *Work out your transportation to and from the place before you start.* A ride from your parents is the safest.

• *Let your parents know where the job is.* Give them the
phone number.

• *Always have the phone numbers of your parents, the police, the fire department, the neighbors, and the children's doctor right by the phone.* Try to have the number of wherever
your employers will be as well.

• *Ask your employers not to arrange for deliveries or service calls when you are there alone.* If they must, ask them to make sure to let you know whom to expect.

• *If you don't feel safe in the house, discuss how to make it safer with your employers.* This should be perfectly possible if you are going to babysit for them regularly. Point out that this is for their children's safety as much as yours.

• *Never let anyone who rings the doorbell or calls know that you are the babysitter.* That advertises that you are alone. If someone calls, say, "I'm afraid Mr. and Mrs. X are busy right now. Can I take a message?"

• *Don't let the children answer the phone or door.* They are easily tricked into letting people in or revealing that you are alone.

• *If you invite a boy over, don't let him think it's an invitation for sex.* Remember, there's no one in the house you can rely on to interrupt or rescue you. Make it clear that your first priority is looking after the children. Always ask your employer if you can have a friend over.

• *Know the address of the house and directions to it by heart.* That way, you can direct the police, fire department, or an ambulance if there's an emergency.

HOW TO HANDLE BABYSITTING EMERGENCIES

• *If you ever have to call an ambulance, the police, or the fire department, give them the address first.* People often forget to do this in their panic.

• *If someone forces his way into the house, or even if you hear suspicious noises, TAKE THE CHILDREN AND GET OUT OF THE HOUSE the back way, if you can.* Go to a neighbor for help. If you can't get out, follow these steps:

1. Call the police if you have time, give them the address, and quickly say, "Someone's breaking in."
2. Go to the Safe Room, if there is one, and lock yourself in. If the children are awake and you can keep them quiet, bring them with you. If there is no Safe Room, follow the other precautions here just the same.
3. Call the neighbors for help. They might be able to frighten the intruder away immediately.
4. DON'T CONFRONT THE INTRUDER.
5. DON'T LEAVE THE CHILDREN UNPROTECTED.

These precautions apply even if you only *think* you hear suspicious noises.

• *If you get a frightening phone call, call your parents and a neighbor immediately.* Sometimes people check to see if you are alone before breaking in.

• *If one of your employers tries to molest you in any way, report him immediately to your parents and never work for him again.* There are many cases of men assaulting the babysitters they hire. Perhaps when the man is driving you home at the end of the evening, he tries to kiss you, puts his hand on your leg, or actually leaps on you and tries rape. Maybe if the mother is away, the father will make a pass at you when he has you alone in his house. Maybe the mother will try something on a boy she's hired. You are in a tricky position because you are younger, alone in their house or car, and intimidated by the fact that they are adults and your employers. If anything like this happens to you, fight back. Use the self-defense techniques described in the next two chapters, and report the adult immediately. Don't let yourself be tricked or embarrassed into keeping the assault a secret; if you do, that adult will probably go on to assault many other teenagers after you.

If your employer just makes you feel uncomfortable, perhaps by looking at you in a sexual way, by talking about sex a lot, by asking you too many personal questions, or by dropping hints that he wants to have "an affair" with you, stop working for that person. Trust your instincts and remember that these behaviors can be preliminaries to sexual assault, a way for him to test you out. If you pretend to ignore him and keep coming back to babysit, he may decide you'll be a compliant victim.

Now you know all the important ways to keep yourself safe in your home, in school, and in other people's homes. You are also armed with the knowledge of what to do if you are ever faced with someone trying to break in. If you refresh your memory of this chapter occasionally, it will help you overcome panic in an emergency. That way, you may be able not only to protect yourself better, but other people as well.

SEVEN

Self-Defense

Most successful self-defense tactics are nonphysical, so don't plan on being able to beat up an assailant once you've read this chapter. Self-defense means what it says: it's about defending yourself, not fighting. The first motto of self-defense is, *The best self-defense is awareness and escape.*

Self-defense methods increase your chances of stopping an assault, but they won't make you invulnerable. Regard the following tactics as a supplement to the self-protection you've already learned.

• *Have faith in your own strength and power.* You are much stronger and faster than you probably know. Most people never test themselves enough to find out what they can really do.

• *Don't believe the popular opinion that no matter what you do, it won't work.* Movies like *Halloween* or *Friday the Thirteenth* perpetuate the myth that teenagers can't be effective when they fight back. That's not true.

• *Think about what you'd do if you were assaulted.* Try to select the methods that would most suit you personally. If you have a strong voice, for example, yelling and

shouting suit you. If you have a weak voice, they don't —
until you practice and make your voice strong.

• *If you ever feel scared, ask yourself why, and think about
what you can do about it.*

• *Whenever possible, try to find an alternative to physical
fighting.* The less contact you have with an assailant, the
safer you'll be.

• *ALWAYS TRUST YOUR INSTINCTS.*

NONPHYSICAL SELF-DEFENSE

You might be surprised to find out how much you and
your body already know about nonphysical self-defense. When we allow our survival instincts to work
without the confusion of rationalizing, guilt, or shame,
those instincts can be mighty smart. Take the story of
this twelve-year-old girl.

I was walking home from school carrying my flute
in its case, when an older boy ran up and tried to
grab it. I just screamed at the top of my lungs. He
got so scared he started to shake, then he ran away.

And the story of this girl of thirteen.

I was in a phone booth and a retarded boy came in
and started hugging me. I don't think he meant any
harm, but it scared me, so I slipped through his arms
and ran home. My body just told me to do it.

And, finally, the story of this sixteen-year-old boy.

I was walking down the street minding my own
business when I vaguely noticed five or six teenage
boys walking in front of me. I didn't pay much attention 'cause there were other people on the street,
but suddenly they spread out over the sidewalk and

when I walked through them, [they] started to hit and kick me. I pushed them aside, dashed ahead, and turned and looked at them and said, "What's the matter with you guys? What are you doing? Are you crazy?" I was so astonished that they would do that, I spoke before I was even scared. They began glaring at me and coming at me, so I said, "I'm not going to fight with you" in a fed-up voice, and turned around and walked away calmly. I was scared by then, but I didn't show it.

These three people, none of whom had been trained, instinctively used the three basic strategies of nonphysical self-defense: the yell, the escape, and the talk.

THE YELL

There's a big difference between the self-defense yell, which some people call the Power Yell, and a regular scream. The yell comes from deep in the stomach, not high in the throat, and is like the yell that a karate or judo master uses before he or she attacks. It's a battle cry, not a frightened screech. It's the sound of anger and attack, not fear.

The yell is designed to do several things: break through that moment when you might be frozen in panic or shock at being attacked, startle the wits out of an attacker, make you look strong and angry instead of weak and scared, and attract attention.

You need to practice the yell. Try it now, into a pillow at home or somewhere after you've warned the people within earshot. Start by thinking of someone or some time that makes you really angry, then yell whatever defiant word or sound comes to mind: "No!" "Stop!" or whatever. If, when you practice it, it makes you feel angry or upset, you're on the right track. If you frighten yourself, even better. The yell is effective with or without words, so use whichever word or sound you find the most powerful for you.

When you use the yell is important — the sooner the better in an attack. If you can yell the instant you sense danger, *before* anyone has his hands on you, you are more likely to frighten off the offender. If you are in a populated area, near people who can hear you, the yell can bring you help. But if you are in an isolated area, the man has already grabbed you, *and you sense that your yell might make him angry or more violent,* then don't do it. As always in self-defense, you'll have to use your own judgment of when to use a particular method.

Often, the yell itself is enough to end an attack. Most molesters who go after people your age aren't expecting anything like a terrifying war cry. Look at the example of these two girls.

> We were playing with a dog in the park, when a man came up to us and began saying obscene things we didn't like. We both instantly did the Power Yell we'd learned right at him. He ran off as fast as he could.

Here's an example of another way a girl used the yell.

> On my block there are a bunch of teenage boys who hang around fixing cars. Every time I walk by them, they yell and whistle at me, even though they know I live here. One day I just couldn't stand it anymore, so I stopped and did a real loud ugly yell at them, then began to point at them and laugh aggressively as if they were the stupidest things I'd ever seen. They all stared at me, utterly silent, in astonishment, as if I'd gone completely mad. Afterwards, I felt shaken but strangely satisfied. And they've never bothered me since.

THE ESCAPE

Like the yell, escape works best when you can act the *instant* you recognize danger. The longer you talk or negotiate with an offender, the harder it will be to get away from him in most circumstances. Experts say there is an instant at the start of an attack when the offender is as uncertain and scared as you. That instant is usually the first moment of approach, when he steps into your path to block your way, for instance, or first says, "Hey, what time is it?" As long as he doesn't have a gun pointed at you, this is the best moment to break away and run.

Escape is often the most successful when it's combined with the yell or with one of the physical forms of self-defense described later. The idea is to stun the offender into paralysis long enough to get away from him, the way this twelve-year-old girl did, according to the following newspaper story from Navarro, California:

> The girl was using a pay-phone in a store one evening with a ten-year-old friend, a boy. Suddenly, she was grabbed by a man who tried to drag her into his car. Both kids did the Power Yell they had learned in self-defense at school, and it stunned the man long enough to enable the girl to break out of his grip. She ran quickly to a nearby house. The police were called and told the direction in which the man was driving away. They caught him speeding and arrested him.

To escape successfully, you have to appraise your situation and look for an escape route. If there is a street behind you, for instance, and an isolated wood ahead of you, you'd want to run into the street, where there are people and houses. If a man grabs you in an isolated area, yelling for help might not work, but if he takes you to a more populated place, then you could yell, "This man is kidnapping me!" or "Get the police!" If you are being attacked by a date, you might have to plan your escape carefully and trick him into going someplace where you can get help. On the other hand, if you are trapped in a car with an offender, your escape might have to be as risky and sudden as opening the door and jumping out.

When the offender is someone in your household, running away might not be possible. The yell might work to stop the assault right at the moment, but talking and telling (see below and chapter eight) are needed to keep it from happening again.

Yelling and running the moment you sense danger are, combined, the most effective way of escaping assault. Even if you're not certain of the danger, don't be afraid to look silly; that's far better than taking a risk.

THE TALK

Your voice can be one of your best weapons, especially when it is coupled with determination. Talking your way out of an attack can be as simple as an outright "No I won't" or as complex as a lengthy persuasion. If, for instance, someone tries to bribe or threaten you into having some kind of sex, an immediate and firm "No" might be enough to dissuade him. Think about how good you are at being firm and direct when you talk to people. Do you look people in the eye, or do you avoid eye contact? Do you speak loudly and clearly, or do you mumble and "um" and "ah"? Do you say what you think right out, or do you usually preface your statements with phrases like "I think," or "I'm sorry, but," or "I guess"? If you are shy or timid at all, practice looking yourself in the eye in a mirror and saying "No" loudly and firmly.

Practice saying no with a friend, too, if you can. One of you could play the offender trying to lure his victim to go home with him. The other can practice resisting the lures with firm answers. Then, switch roles. This is an exercise taught in many self-defense classes. Another exercise is the "broken record" technique. That means saying something like "No I won't" over and over again to every question the offender asks. The conversation you practice with a friend might go like this:

"Look, Louise, you promised to come home with me."

"No, I don't want to."

"But you owe me something. I just bought you dinner."

"No, I don't want to."

"Well I don't believe you. You're just playing hard to get."

"No, I don't want to."

"I'll tell all the other guys you did anyway."

"No, I don't want to."

"Okay, okay, I get the message."

If you find this kind of rudeness difficult, remember that you have the right to be rude and unhelpful if you ever sense any danger to yourself.

For some offenders, even a strong, persistent "No" doesn't work. It may, for example, only make them more angry and violent. If you see this happening, you will probably have to change your strategy from a simple firm refusal to something more complicated. That's what Celia found when she was walking home one night.

It was late, the street was deserted, and I was by myself, so I already felt kind of nervous. Suddenly, this weird-looking guy drove by on a motorcycle, saw me, and swerved his bike around. He drove right up on the sidewalk in front of me and stopped. He looked pretty crazy and I knew I was in trouble. Then he began insulting me and saying things like "What's a nice Jewish girl like you doing out so late?"

I could tell getting mad or huffy wasn't going to help, so I pretended I didn't understand what he meant. Instead, I said something like "What a great bike you've got. Boy, am I glad you came along, 'cause I was feeling scared." He looked interested, so I kept going. "You know, there are some kinds of guys who are so desperate they'd jump a girl out alone, but I could tell immediately you aren't like that. You probably have your pick of girls!" I went on like that, and even though what I was saying sounded ridiculous to me, he began to look proud. He didn't really look anything like a nice guy, but I guess no one had ever said such things to him before. In the end, he let me go without touching me.

If Celia had been able to run somewhere safe, yell for help, or in any other way escape quickly, she would have taken less of a risk, but as it was she could tell those methods wouldn't work fast enough. So, with her mind racing, she found words that defused his anger and turned him into a protector instead of an assailant. When you are attacked, however, you have no idea whether you have the type of rapist who can be talked out of raping or the type whom talk will only enrage. To find out, you have to test him by saying something like

Wow, I can tell you are really upset. Someone must have done something terrible to make you feel like that. I'm pretty scared, but maybe we could work something out that would make you feel better.

If he responds to this with interest, or even if he just calms down, you may have the type who can be tricked. If so, keep talking along those lines while you figure out a way to escape. Rapists are egomaniacs, so remember these two rules:

• *Keep the attention focused on him* with words like "What's made you so upset?"

• *Keep yourself human in his eyes* with phrases like "This is scary for me, but maybe we can work it out."

Once you've maneuvered him into a place or position that's safer for you, use one of these tactics:

• *Make a sudden physical self-defense move* (see below) *and run.*

• *Yell and escape.*

• *Trick or persuade him into letting you go.* Say something like "Just let me go to the bathroom," or "I'll just go back to the party to find some booze."

If your talking is making the attacker more angry, you'll be able to tell fast enough, so stop. The more angry he is, the more liable he is to hurt you. If you can't talk yourself out of an attack, can't trick the attacker, or can't escape, you may have to resort to the physical self-defense methods described below.

Verbal resistance often works best with people you know. If the offender is someone in your household or a boyfriend, the yell, a firm "No," and a threat to tell can effectively stop the abuse. If your uncle tries to "French kiss" you, for example, the yell will probably stop him. If your grandfather puts his hands down your pants, a yell or a "No" loud and clear could get that hand out fast. If a boyfriend pins you down and tries to force sex, a sincere threat to tell might stop him. One girl who had been molested by her father every night for years finally put a stop to it by using a simple method she'd learned in a self-defense class: When he opened the door to her bedroom, she said loudly and cheerfully for the whole house to hear, "What do you want, Dad?" He quietly left the room and never came to molest her again.

If the nonphysical strategies don't work with the people you know, or you are too scared to use them, read the next chapter, "Getting Help."

PHYSICAL SELF-DEFENSE

The idea of women or teenagers defending themselves against a sexual attack makes a lot of people angry. For years, the police have been advising against it in the mistaken belief that women and young people can't fight grown men, so would only put themselves in more danger if they tried. The message has been "Lie back and take it passively so you won't get hurt," an idea that ignores the fact that sexual assault itself hurts very much.

Several studies have been done over the years on whether physical resistance can help a woman escape a rape attack. The results have on the whole been encouraging. Women who combined yelling and running away escaped the most, but many who fought back escaped, too. Those who fought tended to be injured in minor ways, with bruises and cuts, but those who tried no form of resistance were almost always raped. Not everyone who resisted succeeded, however. Sometimes fighting with the rapist got a woman too injured to resist anymore, and she was raped. Sometimes her struggles made the rapist get even more violent. Only you can decide whether to resist a sexual attack or not, and your decision has to depend on these questions:

• *Does the attacker have a weapon?* If he has a gun, resistance is not usually wise. If he has a knife, there might be opportunities to get the knife away from him or to escape if he puts it down, but resistance without proper training in self-defense is difficult and risky. The good news is that only about a third of attackers use weapons — probably even fewer than that among those who attack kids and teenagers.

• *How capable do you feel of resisting?* A timid struggle or half-hearted attempt to hit the attacker won't help. You have to feel angry and powerful.

• *How dangerous is the immediate situation?* If you are within earshot of people, resistance could work. If you can run somewhere safe quickly, you are better off, too. Once you've been dragged off to somewhere isolated, your chances of escape are much worse.

• *Have you had training in self-defense?* If you have, your chances of resisting successfully are stronger. See your phone book and the back of this book for places that teach self-defense.

There are only a few physical self-defense moves that can be taught safely in a book. Most need to be taught and practiced in a class. In order to be able to use them in the midst of the panic you'll feel when attacked, you have to *physically* practice them so much that they become second nature. This is true of the moves taught here, too. Practice them, don't just sit in a comfortable chair reading about them. You can practice them with friends, parents, brothers and sisters, or even on pillows, but practice only with people you feel comfortable with. A major benefit of learning self-defense is gaining confidence, so if you practice with an older brother who always ends up sitting on you, that's not going to work — you'll just feel a failure. Also, remember that physical self-defense is serious and should never be used in a playful fight with friends. And don't forget that every physical move is enhanced if it can be accompanied by a blood-freezing Power Yell.

THE STAND

To give you power behind any kind of physical move, you need to be well balanced on your feet. Stand with your legs a shoulder-width apart, your hips balanced comfortably — not thrust too far forward or back — and your back straight but relaxed. Put one foot somewhat in front of the other so that you can't be pushed off balance easily. Have a friend push you until you find the right balance that keeps you steady. Now, keep your head up and your arms up and out, one in front of your face to protect it and one in front of your stomach. This position is also known as "the fighter's stance."

THE SCRAPE

The scrape is an extension of the kick, and is best used if you are attacked from behind. First you do a sharp backward kick into the offender's kneecap, then you scrape your heel down his shin.

THE KICK

The kick is best to use because it keeps you at the farthest distance from the offender. Kick from the knee only, with a sharp forward action. Keep your toes up and snap your leg back immediately. *Don't kick your whole leg* and *don't leave your leg sticking out after the kick.* That makes it too easy for someone to grab it and tip you over. Think of the word *snap* when you kick.

The kick works no matter how small you are because you can always reach an adult's knee or shin. Aim at the knee for most effect.

A California school reported an incident in which a ten-year-old girl named Ginny used the kick and the yell with great success.

She had just finished going to the bathroom when a strange man pushed open the door to her stall and tried to grab her. She immediately did the special self-defense yell and kicked him very hard in the shins. This stunned him long enough for her to be able to get past him and out into the hallway, where she called for help. The man fled the school with a teacher in pursuit. Although he got away, Ginny was safe.

Ginny used the right combination of self-defense strategies: the yell, the kick, the escape, and asking for help.

THE ELBOW HIT

This can be used for attacks from behind and beside you. Swivel around so that you are standing slightly sideways compared to the assailant. Thrust your arm forward quickly, fist clenched and facing upward. Then bend your arm and thrust quickly backward with your elbow pointed into the offender's groin or stomach. The harder you do it and the straighter your elbow goes back, the more power you'll have. Now *practice*.

An assault prevention class reported the successful use of both the instep stomp and elbow hit by two of their students:

Twelve-year-old Tanya and her eight-year-old brother, Marcus, were walking home from school when two teenage boys, fifteen and sixteen, grabbed Tanya and tried to drag her off the sidewalk into a yard. In telling about this, Tanya said in a matter-of-fact manner, "So we just started doing what you taught us. I hit the first one in the stomach with my elbow and stomped on his instep. My brother hit the second one from behind. Both of us did our yells." This was not at all what the attackers expected, and they ran off.

THE PALM HEEL

Hold your hand up and out, palm forward and fingers pointed upward. Your wrist should be bent back so that the palm of your hand faces outward. Keep your fingers slightly bent and close together and your thumb next to your fingers so it doesn't get hurt. Aim at the underside of the attacker's nose or chin, and thrust hard and quick up into it with the heel of your hand. Most teenagers can reach an adult's nose or chin, and you can hurt and stun someone long enough to escape from him this way. You are very unlikely to break his nose, if that worries you.

THE INSTEP STOMP

Lift your knee high and stomp down as hard as you can on the top of the offender's foot. You can use this whether he is facing you, behind you, or beside you.

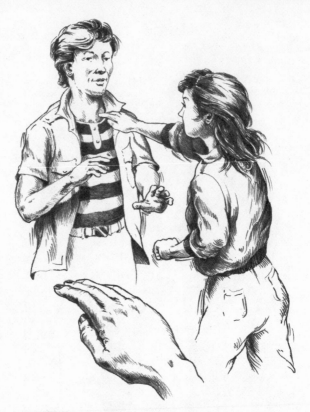

THE SPEARHAND EYE AND THROAT POKE

Hold your hand out straight and firm, wrist straight, fingers bent slightly at the tips. Tuck your thumb into your palm so it's out of the way. This position is called the spearhand. It can be used to thrust hard and straight into an attacker's throat or eyes, depending on how high you can reach. (You will be able to reach if he picks you up.) If you hit him in the throat, it will cause temporary breathing difficulty — enough to give you some time to run. If you hit him in the eyes, you will hurt and daze him long enough to escape. You will not permanently blind him. It's hard to imagine poking someone in the eyes, but if you let yourself imagine doing it to a rapist, you might be able to actually do it if you ever need to.

BREAKING A HOLD

If someone has his hands around your mouth from behind to prevent you from screaming, the best way to get out of it is to grab his little fingers and snap them backward. You can only do this if you have your hands free, of course, but it will hurt him enough to make him let go. Most people try to grab the assailant's arms, but that doesn't work.

If someone has his arm around your neck from behind, turn your head into his elbow. That way, you'll relieve the pressure from your throat so you can breathe. Then try the backward kick, shin scrape, and instep stomp. A self-defense teacher told of how Michael, a boy of only eight, fought off two attackers with these methods. He had learned them in a few self-defense classes he'd taken with his mother.

One day when Michael was playing in his front yard, he was approached by a man drinking beer. The man had candy and a BB gun. He said, "Do you want some candy?" Michael said, "I don't talk to strangers," as he'd been taught, and backed away. Then the man said, "Do you want to look at my BB gun?" Michael again said, firmly, "No."

Suddenly, Michael saw a second man, also drinking beer. He stood behind Michael. The first man grabbed Michael, dragged him between two parked cars on the street, and started to molest him. Michael planted his feet to get his balance, kicked the man in the shin, scraped down his assailant's shin with his foot, stomped on his instep, did his yell, broke free, and ran to his neighbor's for help. The two men ran off in the other direction.

When the director of the self-defense program came to visit Michael at home after this, she found him shaken but proud of himself. The first thing he said to her was, "I did good, Marsha!"

If an eight-year-old boy can fight off two men after only a few self-defense lessons, imagine what you can do!

The story of Michael illustrates something else about self-defense, too. When you have succeeded in fighting someone off, or even if you know you tried, you can feel very good about yourself. You are a proud survivor.

IF YOU CAN'T ESCAPE

If you are attacked and can't escape no matter what, there are still ways you can protect yourself. Even if you are raped, there are things you can do during the rape that will help you survive it.

• *Take a few deep breaths.* These calm you down and help you recover from that first moment of panic. When you are calm, you can think clearly, and that helps you to survive.

• *Examine the situation.* Can you see an escape route? Can you persuade the attacker to put down his weapon by saying something like "Look, I'll do what you say, you don't need that. It's just making me nervous." Can you throw the weapon out of his reach if he does put it down?

• *Look at the attacker's face,* if you can. Try to remember what he looks like, what he's wearing, how he talks, how he smells. This will help to catch and identify him later.

• *Keep thinking about how to escape.* Even if you have to submit to the assault, you'll want to get away as fast as you can afterwards. And perhaps, during the assault, the attacker will leave his face vulnerable to an eye or nose poke.

There are two final methods of self-defense that can be used during an actual assault. The first is the eye gouge — you put your hands on either side of the attacker's face, then suddenly push your thumbs into his eyes. This won't blind him, but it'll put him in enough pain to let you go. The second is the testicle squeeze — you take hold of his testicles and twist with as much force as you can. This could even knock him out. These two methods are very hard for most people to do because they can only be done when you are physically close to the attacker, because they seem so gruesome, and because if they aren't done with enough force, they may only enrage the attacker. Think now about whether you might ever be willing to use these techniques. During an attack, when your survival instincts are working, you may be willing to do anything to save yourself.

EIGHT

Getting Help

Being sexually assaulted is like being tortured. The assailant usually makes you undress, as does a torturer. He touches, hits, squeezes, or penetrates the most private parts of your body — your buttocks, your breasts, your vagina, your penis — against your will. He taunts you like a torturer with dirty names and cruel personal comments. He does everything he can to make you feel small and ugly and humiliated. And sometimes he forces you to do sexual things to him, like suck his penis, or rub him, or masturbate him. He uses you like a piece of rag.

And people call this "sexy"? They do. And because they do, victims of assault are often too ashamed to ever tell anyone that it happened to them. They feel as if they'd be confessing something as private and embarrassing as their fantasies while masturbating.

A lot of us won't accept that sexual assault is a kind of torture — we all prefer not to look unpleasant things in the face — so we tell ourselves that rape doesn't hurt, that sexual abuse is no worse than a dirty movie, and that there's a lot more fuss about it these days than there needs to be. Even if you don't believe you have these attitudes, you might find yourself thinking that you don't deserve help after an assault. You might blame yourself for what happened.

But anyone who has been sexually assaulted in any way needs help. Assault is an abnormal, terrifying event, and you should not be expected to cope with it on your own.

This chapter is essential whether you have been assaulted or not, because it explains why you should *never* be too ashamed to tell, no matter what happens to you. And it explains why you deserve help, and how to get it.

The best way to help yourself recover from an assault is to turn to someone you love for sympathy. Many studies have found that people who can talk about the assault and who get sympathy and support from those close to them recover much better than people who keep the whole thing secret. So if you think you should keep your assault quiet so that you don't upset anyone or make them mad, think again. It would be much more upsetting for anyone who loves you, and for you yourself, to see you burdened by a terrible secret than to have it out in the open.

First of all, you must know that whatever has happened to you, you are not a failure. Although this book is mostly about protecting yourself, being assaulted doesn't mean you've failed. Maybe it happened before you knew about self-defense; maybe it happened because nothing could have stopped it. If you are afraid to seek help because you think you brought on the assault yourself, stop thinking like that now. You are not at fault, you are not a failure. You have a right to get all the help and sympathy you need.

YOUR REACTIONS TO SEXUAL ASSAULT

During a sexual attack, most people think only of one thing: "Am I going to die?" You are either afraid the assailant will murder you, or that he will badly hurt or mutilate you. Some people freeze with fear during an attack and cannot even remember what happened afterward, other people find their minds racing and their memories clear. Your body does strange things when it is in terrible danger: adrenaline floods through you, your heart pumps wildly, and you alternate between feeling you can't breathe to panting too fast (which is why taking a few deep breaths helps so much). Some people feel numb, others feel electric with panic.

Right after an attack of any kind, you are going to be in shock. Every person has his or her own way of reacting to shock, and lots of people react in different ways all in a row. One minute, for instance, you may feel calm and relieved, the next in such a panic you can't catch your breath. Some people cry and scream and shake, some people remain icily calm. Some people are stunned, some active. Many find their emotions swinging wildly from one extreme to the next. Some people are horrified to find they feel a strange gratitude to the assailant for leaving them alive. A lot of victims think they have literally gone mad.

A little later, you might find yourself almost as frightened by your reactions to the assault as by the assault itself. Suddenly you are full of terrors — scared of the dark, of men, of being alone, of certain places. You may have nightmares and trouble eating or sleeping for a while. You may get sudden shakes and fears one minute, then feel calm and coldly indifferent the next. "Am I going crazy?" you may wonder. "What is happening to me?"

What is happening is that you are having a normal

reaction to an extremely abnormal event. Everyone has these reactions and you are not alone or weird to be feeling the way you do. People who've lived through other traumas, like fires and accidents, have the same kinds of reactions. You have been through a terrible experience and you will need time to get over it. As Karen, the girl who was raped in the park, said:

> The counselor I went to told me, "One day, this will be a thing that happened to you and not a major tragedy." I thought, "How insensitive. She doesn't understand." But I realized today that it's been three years and now it *is* just a thing that happened. As my mother put it, I had to go through a period of mourning.

It may take as long as three years before the assault is "just something that happened," but it probably won't take that long for you to be able to get back to a normal, happy state of being. You won't forget the assault — no one can — but you will find a way of living without letting it dominate your life. Most people take between three months and a year to get over the fears and depression an assault causes. That may seem like a long time, but you *will* get through it. Almost everybody does.

WHOM TO TELL ABOUT INCEST

If you are being sexually assaulted by your father or another family member, you have two major tasks to accomplish: to stop the assaults, and to recover from them.

If you have the courage and strength, you might be able to stop the assaults by using the yell and the talk discussed in the chapter on self-defense, but the situation is probably too complicated and frightening for such a simple solution. Most likely you will need to get someone else's help. Here are the possibilities to consider:

• *Can you tell a sister or brother?* Sometimes the offender is molesting all the children in the family and they are keeping it secret from each other. If your sister, for example, has been molested too, it might be easier for both of you to seek help together than for either of you to do it alone.

• *Can you tell your mother (or, if she is the offender, your father)?* You may have avoided telling your mother for reasons like these: "She already knows about the abuse and doesn't care"; "She'd be too shocked or frightened to help"; "She wouldn't believe me"; "She'd blame me and be furious"; "She doesn't love me." Sometimes these reasons are valid, but sometimes they aren't. Think carefully about whether you are being fair to your mother. Would it help to give her the appendix for parents in the back of this book to read? Would it help to get another adult you trust to tell her? Are you sure that her fear of facing the truth would be stronger than her desire to protect you?

It is true that the news will be a shock to your mother. If she loves your father, stepfather, whoever he is, she's going to hurt a lot when she finds out what he's been doing to you. She might get angry at you at first. She might not want to believe you because she can't face the truth. She's going to feel betrayed by him, maybe disgusted by him. And she's going to be shattered at what's happened to her family. On top of all this, she's going to have to decide whether to tell the police and whether to leave him. For these reasons, you might want to turn to someone other than your mother at first. Remember, though, that she's going to have to know in the end, and that she can end up being more of a help and comfort to you than anyone else in the world.

• *Which other adults could you tell first?* If you think your mother would be too upset, wouldn't believe you, or would get angry with you, another adult who does believe you can help to calm her down and comfort both of you. Could you tell a friend's mother, perhaps? A teacher or a doctor? Another relative, like an aunt? That person, with your permission, could either tell your mother or help you decide what to do next. This was the case for Betsy, as told by a self-defense teacher:

> Whenever Betsy was alone with her grandfather, he began to talk about the sexual acts he wanted to do with her. He also tried to bribe her to kiss and hug him. She became more and more scared, and finally told a self-defense teacher at school about it. Betsy said, "I love my grandfather and my family does too, so I can't tell them."
>
> The teacher asked Betsy if she could call her mother so that all three of them could talk about it. Betsy agreed, and her mother was very understanding and concerned. She believed Betsy, listened carefully to everything she said, and then decided to tell the grandfather to stop. She also decided that Betsy would no longer be left alone with him.

• *Can you tell a friend?* If you have a close friend whom you trust, you might find it easier to go to an adult with her help. This happened to Jennifer when she finally decided to tell a self-defense teacher about her abuse. The teacher said,

> Jennifer came to get help because her father had been sexually abusing her for years. With her came her best friend, Luisa, who knew all about the abuse.

As Jennifer told her story, there were times when she cried so hard she couldn't speak. Each time, Luisa picked up the story, explaining what had happened and encouraging Jennifer to go on. With the help of her friend, Jennifer was able to do something she might not have been able to do alone.

If a friend of yours is being abused, you can be like Luisa and help her or him tell an adult.

• *Can you call a professional counselor for help?* A rape crisis hotline or a children's protection agency are two places where you can find help. There is a list of places to call beginning on page 134, but first you'll probably have several important questions you'll want answered.

If I tell a professional counselor, or any adult for that matter, will the police have to know?

As long as you hide your real name, address, and phone number, the police will not be informed. In some states, adults who work with minors (people under eighteen) are legally obliged to tell the police about any sexual abuse that comes to their attention, as long as they have the victim's name. If you don't want the police to know yet, don't give your real name immediately and first ask a rape crisis center what the policy is in your state.

If I tell a professional counselor, will my family be told?

Most centers that deal with sexual assault keep all their cases entirely confidential. They won't tell anyone against your will, even your parents. If you want to make doubly sure, call the center and ask about their policy before you give them your name or story. Again, you can refuse to give your name or use a fake one.

If I tell and the police find out, will my father (or whoever the offender is) go to prison?

Not necessarily. In some states there are organizations called child protective services or child protection agencies. Their job is to talk to the family, find out what the problem is, and look at all the possible solutions that can keep the family together and avoid arrest, if that's what you want. If you and your family don't want the offender to go to prison, it's unlikely that he will, for your cooperation will be needed to prove him guilty.

If I tell and the authorities find out, will I be taken away from my family?

In some cases yes, although usually you won't be taken away forever. You can find out the likelihood of this by calling your local rape crisis center and asking for advice. In New York State, for example, there is a Child Abuse Hotline; if abuse is detected, the procedure is to remove the child from the home immediately. If you want to be removed for your own safety, fine, but if you don't, you should keep your name and address quiet until you are advised of the law in your area. If you are removed, you are usually put in an institution or a foster home until you can go back home, and you may be there for several months.

If I tell, will my family hate me?

Not if you find a counselor to explain to your family what is happening and why they should be on your side. Some offenders hate what they are doing and are glad to get some help with stopping it. At first your family probably will be upset, and maybe even tend to blame you, but in the end they will most likely be grateful. Give your family the appendix for parents in the back of this book and get the help of a rape crisis or child abuse counselor to help them find the right attitude.

PLACES TO CALL FOR RESCUE FROM
FAMILY ABUSE

RAPE HOTLINE

This number, usually listed on the front page of your phone book or under "rape" in the *R* section, will put you in touch with a rape crisis center. These centers have counselors who are trained to help the victims of incest and family abuse. The help is absolutely confidential — you just talk on the phone or arrange to go in to see them, and they won't even tell your parents if you don't want them to. Counselors can also advise you on what other steps to take to stop the abuse and get help recovering from it. Counselors have met countless people in your position; they'll sympathize with you, they'll believe you, and they'll do all they can to help.

NATIONAL RUNAWAY HOTLINE,
1-800-231-6946 (toll-free
everywhere except Texas);
1-800-392-3352 (toll-free in Texas)

Many victims of sexual abuse at home run away to escape from it. This can put you in all sorts of other dangers — from people who want to turn you into a prostitute, from rapists, from drug pushers, from people who like to hurt kids. The Runaway Hotline, which you can call for free at any time of day or night, *whether you've run away yet or not,* will put you in touch with someone who can give you advice on where to stay in your area, how to get help for family problems and incest, and where to get help for sexual assault, pregnancy, drug problems, drinking problems, and suicidal urges.

CHILD PROTECTION SERVICES/AGENCIES

If you want immediate rescue from your home, this is the number to call. Look up Child Abuse Hotline on the first page of your phone book, or call Information for the number of your local child protection service. Or, turn to your local government pages (often at the front or back of the phone book in a different color than the rest of it) and look up Social Services under *S*. In this category there should be a heading something like "Children's Services" or "Child Maltreatment/Abuse Reports." That's the number to call.

ALA-TEEN/AL-ANON OR ALCOHOLICS ANONYMOUS (AA)

If you have an alcoholic parent who is abusing you, these organizations can help. Look them up under the *A* section of your phone book, or call Information.

For other places to find help, see "Sources for Safety" in the back of this book.

WHAT TO DO AFTER A SEXUAL ASSAULT

When you've been molested or sexually assaulted, your first priority is your own safety. This is the order of action you should take:

• *Go somewhere safe.* If you were attacked outside, get away from the attacker and the place it happened as soon as possible. Go to a store, the police, a hospital, a friend's house, your home — whichever is nearest and safest. If you were attacked at home, you might want to get out. At the same time, you shouldn't be alone and vulnerable on the streets. So, as soon as you can, get to a phone and call for someone to come get you.

• *Decide whom to call.* Your mother? A friend? The police? An ambulance? Most teenagers either call their parents immediately or keep the assault a secret from everyone, not seeking help at all. You should seek help right away because you are going to feel terrified. You need and deserve comfort. If you really think telling your mother or father would make everything worse, think of someone else you can turn to right now. An older sister or brother? Another relative? A friend or the parent of a friend? If you are certain your family couldn't handle the news, or that you couldn't stand their reactions to it, you may want to turn to a rape crisis center instead, at least for the time being. This was the choice Karen, the girl mentioned earlier, made after she was raped.

> I didn't want to tell my mom. I guess I felt too guilty 'cause I was buying drugs from the guy who raped me. So I didn't tell anyone for a couple of days, I just stayed home. Then I heard about a rape crisis center on the radio, and I just went right to the phone and called them. The lady on the phone asked me if I was okay and I said I was still bleeding, so she told me to come in. They were real nice. They said I could use a fake name if I didn't want my mother to know, they never made me tell the police, and they got a woman doctor to examine me and give me medicine. I got counseling there, too, and kind of made friends with them.

You'll probably want to have someone with you right after the assault to see you through the hospital, the police, telling your family, and those first terrible hours when you are so shaken and scared. No one likes to be alone after an assault. On the other hand, you may, like the fifteen-year-old daughter of this woman, want to cope with almost everything yourself.

When my daughter was raped, she stayed real calm about it. She told me, but she insisted on going to the hospital and telling the police on her own. She was so grown-up and capable about it, I was amazed.

After a sexual assault, you need to take back control over your life as soon as possible. For some people, that means making their own decisions and coping with everything on their own. If you are able to do that, it can help you to heal. But don't deny yourself help just to look heroic.

• *Decide whether to tell the police.* If you tell the police immediately, the advantage is that they'll be able to gather evidence of the assault right away, which will help them catch and prosecute the man who did it. They will also be more prone to believe you. On the other hand, the police can seem gruff, unsympathetic, and scary right after you've been assaulted. They may make you tell the story over and over again until you feel as if they're trying to trick you (they are actually just making sure they have the story right and trying to get you to remember every single detail that might help their investigation), and they may act hurried, indifferent, and callous. This is often because they *are* hurried and they have heard countless cases of sexual abuse, but it's also because you are in an especially sensitive frame of mind right now: everyone seems brutal and frightening.

If you decide not to tell the police right away, you can still do it later. They won't be happy about this, but it's better to report assault late than not at all. Many people don't go to the police right away because they don't trust them, don't like them, and are afraid of not being believed. Usually, the police are sympathetic to teenagers who've been assaulted, but sometimes they do seem to snicker at you or shout at you or treat you badly. It's therefore always a good idea to have a parent, close friend, or rape crisis counselor with you when you talk to the police. People like this can help support you, comfort you, and protect you from tactless questions and mistreatment.

When you report sexual assault to the police, you'll do it either at a hospital, at the police station, or at home. The police will ask you to tell them exactly what happened. They'll want you to tell them who abused you, what he looked like, what he wore, what he smelled like, whether you knew him before, how you met him, how he approached you — every detail. They'll want to know every detail of what he did to you, too, no matter how embarrassing. They may take pictures of you, especially if you are bruised, disheveled, or otherwise hurt.

All the questions the police may ask you about what happened and who the assailant was are valid and should be answered truthfully. But if they ask anything like "Did you enjoy it?" "Do you like the guy?" "Have you had sex with him before?" you don't have to answer. These questions are not only irrelevant, they are insulting.

No one can promise that going to the police is pleasant. But reporting an assault is the only way the assailant is going to get caught, and the only way he's going to be stopped from doing it to someone else.

If you are worried about the consequences of telling the police — that you'll be removed from your family, that someone you love might get arrested — call your local rape crisis center and ask them about the laws on this in your area. *And remember, telling the police does not oblige you to testify in a trial.*

• *If you know the offender, decide how best to stop his assaults.* When you are sexually assaulted by someone you know, especially someone you know well, it's much harder to decide whom to tell about it, or whether to tell anyone at all. If he is your best friend's brother, for instance, you may not want to go to the police because you don't want to bring misery to his family. If he is your sister's husband, you might think that no one would believe you if you told. If he's a boyfriend, you may tell yourself that the assault only happened because you led him on. You cannot blame yourself for the assault. Anyone who forces any kind of sex on you is dangerous. You would do him and his family a big favor in the long run to tell the truth now, when it still might be possible to get help for him. If you can't think of anyone to tell, go to a rape crisis center and ask them for help. Rape crisis centers aren't only for people who've been raped, but for people who've been sexually assaulted in any way.

• *Decide whether to go to a hospital.* You should go if the assault has physically damaged you in any way, if you are in shock, in any kind of pain, or if you've been raped. Going to a hospital right after a rape allows a doctor to gather evidence that will make convicting the rapist easier if he is caught.

Rapists often spread venereal diseases, so you should get tests and treatment for that (although you don't need to take a VD test until about a week after the assault). If you are afraid of getting pregnant from the rape, a hospital can test you for that, too, and help you with the consequences. Pregnancy from rape is a risk, but a small one — it only happens in 3 to 5 percent of all rapes. Pregnancy tests are done by taking a sample of your blood or urine.

If you do go to a hospital right away, be prepared for a long wait. You will be sent to the emergency room, and you may be kept there for two hours or more if there are a lot of accidents and heart attacks that day. Emergency rooms are depressing places, even worse when you are in a state of shock, so don't go alone. Bring a parent, a friend, or a rape crisis counselor with you.

Once a doctor is ready, you will be examined. If you are a girl and you have been raped, you'll be given a pelvic examination. If you are a boy and have been raped or assaulted in another way, your penis, rectum, and mouth might be examined. The doctor will also look your body over for other signs of assault, like bruises and scratches.

If you are a girl and have not had a pelvic exam before, tell the doctor so that he or she can explain to you what is happening and why. A good doctor should do this anyway, but in case he or she doesn't, this is what to expect:

You are told to undress from the waist down, and you are given a gown to wear. Then you lie on the examining table with your knees up and your feet placed apart and in stirrups. This position enables the doctor to see in your vagina. The doctor will then insert a metal or plastic instrument called a speculum into your vagina, which gently opens it so that he or she can see if you've been hurt there. The doctor will take a dab of tissue from inside you with a cotton swab, which will feel like a quick scrape if you feel it at all, to be tested later in the lab for signs of VD and samples of the attacker's sperm or skin. The doctor may also examine your anus for tears and the outside of your body for scratches, cuts, and bruises.

Under normal circumstances, a pelvic exam rarely hurts, although it is never exactly pleasant. But after a sexual assault, it can be frightening and a little painful. For this reason, you might prefer to go to a family doctor instead of an emergency room. The other alternative is to ask a rape crisis center for the hospital nearest you with a rape crisis unit, so that you can get a doctor trained in dealing with people in your situation. If you want a woman doctor, ask for one. Not every place will be able to provide one, but some will. And let your friend, parent, or counselor either hold your hand during the examination, or, if you'd rather, just wait outside until it's over.

COPING WITH PARENTS

The first problem that comes up with parents is whether to tell them about your assault. The trouble with *not* telling them is that you'll have to keep up an act all the time. When you get depressed or afraid, you'll either have to hide it or invent a reason to explain your mood. If you have some of the other common reactions — fear of going out, loss of appetite, fear of going to school or seeing friends — your parents are going to notice. And if they don't know what's wrong, they are going to ask you over and over again to explain. Unless you are absolutely certain that your parents will refuse to even try to understand sexual assault and that they are bound to make your life hell, give them the appendix for parents section of this book and tell them what happened to you. You need their help and support, for they can encourage your recovery more than anyone else. They can help you feel good about yourself again, make you feel loved and protected again, and help you get back your faith in the good side of life. If you need to tell them with the help of another friend, a rape counselor, or a teacher, do. In the end, it will be worth it.

Here are some of the main reasons you may *not* want to tell your parents, and what to do about them:

• *I'm afraid they'll get mad at me, blame me, or punish me for getting assaulted.* If they say something like "How could you let this happen to you?" or "I *told* you not to go to that place!" or if they try to punish you for the assault, try talking to them with the help of an adult friend, teacher, or counselor who's on your side. You could also try giving them the appendix for parents at the back of this book. If this isn't enough, tell them that if they want to help you get better, they should talk to a rape crisis counselor. They need to understand that what happened to you wasn't your fault.

• *I'm too embarrassed to discuss anything as intimate as sexual assault with them.* Being embarrassed is not enough of a reason to deny yourself the help your parents can give you. If you don't want to go into the specific details of what was done to you, you don't have to. But your sense of privacy and their prudishness just aren't important in the face of an emergency like this. Try to remember that sexual assault is primarily a crime of violence, not sex; what's important is that you were hurt and frightened.

• *I'm just getting my own privacy and independence apart from my parents; I don't want to undo that by involving them in this assault.* It is especially traumatic to be assaulted when you are just experimenting with a little freedom. It can make you feel as if you're being punished for trying to grow up. But even though the assault will make you scared for a while, even though it makes it more difficult to trust people, it won't stop you from becoming independent. If, for now, you need to retreat into the nest of your family again — that's fine. Even adults usually want to be coddled and comforted when something bad happens, and families are supposed to give us comfort and support. Don't give up on your independence. Don't let your excitement about the world and all its possibilities get spoiled by your assault. But for now, do let yourself be protected if that's what you need. You have a whole life of independence before you, and although you'll be feeling more timid for a while, the assault won't stop you from growing up strong.

• *I don't want to upset and hurt my parents.* This is a noble sentiment, but not appropriate right now. It would hurt most parents a lot more to see you upset but not know what's wrong, or to find out years later what happened and know they'd never had the chance to help you, than to hear the truth now.

• *I don't want them to find out what I was doing when the assault happened.* If you were doing something you weren't supposed to when you were assaulted, like buying drugs, drinking, or seeing someone your parents don't like, you may be afraid your parents will blame you or punish you. You or a counselor should remind them that breaking rules is not the same as inviting an assault. Ask yourself whether your prediction of their attitude is accurate. Would your parents really be mad about what you were doing, or just concerned about whether you are all right?

• *I'm afraid to tell because my assailant threatened to kill me if I do.* A lot of rapists and molesters use threats and lies to keep their victims quiet. "I'll kill you or your sister." "Your mother gave me permission to do this to you." "If you tell, your mother will kill herself." "I'm having an affair with your mother — you want your father to find out?" Whatever the lie, try not to believe it. Remember, the molester is a criminal and he's trying to protect himself from getting caught. And if he's using threats, ask yourself how likely it really is that he could carry them out. Does he really know where you live and who you are? Would he really risk exposing himself by seeking revenge on you? If you think there is a real danger, talk to a rape crisis counselor or the police about what to do to protect yourself and your family until the offender is arrested.

Once your parents do know about your assault, there will still be problems. Even the most understanding of parents will probably make mistakes. They may try to overprotect you — they'll want to keep you in, impose a curfew, go everywhere with you, know where you've been. Some parents might not actually do these things, but they'll want to. If you see this happening, remind yourself of how bad they feel about your assault. Because they couldn't protect you from the assault, they feel as if they've failed as parents. They may hate themselves for it. Assure them that you understand this, but that the assault has not made you or your needs different. You need to grow up and you need to be independent. With all you've learned about protecting yourself, you'll be able to do that more safely.

Another problem is that you'll probably be furious at your parents on some level for not rescuing you from the assault. You may feel, like them, that they've failed to be good parents. Although this is perfectly understandable, it isn't fair. As explained earlier, the assault is only one person's fault: the offender's. Your parents can't hover over you all the time, and you wouldn't want them to.

If you are sexually assaulted, your parents, especially your father, may react with such horror and embarrassment that they withdraw from you. The sexual nature of the assault might make your father feel alienated or shy. Brothers and female members of the family might withdraw like this, too. This makes it harder for you to recover because it makes your assault seem like a dirty secret. You all need to be reminded that there is nothing to be ashamed of. Regard it as an accident, like a car crash, if it helps.

Your father (or brother) might also react by wanting to hunt the offender down. This doesn't help you either, because instead of focusing on you and giving you the sympathy you need, he is getting into imaginary or potentially real fights with your assailant. That leaves you out in the cold.

If any of these problems become more than you can cope with, which is not unusual, you and your family should go to a rape crisis center. The counselors are familiar with these kinds of troubles and know how to help you talk to each other and sort them out.

COPING WITH FRIENDS

Choosing which friends to tell, if any, is extremely difficult. A lot of your friends won't know much about sexual assault — some may not even know what it is. The whole subject will probably embarrass them, make them blush and giggle, and then maybe make them shy away from you. It's important, therefore, to think carefully about whom to tell.

If you decide not to tell anyone, you will again be faced with a very lonely time. Carrying around a secret like that makes you feel different from everyone else and shut off from them, as if you're locked behind a glass pane. This is especially true if the assaults are still happening to you. So, look over your friends. Would any of them be sympathetic? Can you trust any of them not to go blabbing the news all over school? If the answer to these two questions is no, you may well have to keep the assault a secret within your family, or between your family and a counselor. At least, that is, until your friends become a little more sophisticated.

If you do have any friends you could tell, give them this book to read. It'll not only help them understand what you've been through, they'll learn how to protect themselves, too. But don't be surprised if they are embarrassed for a while, or if they make insensitive remarks like "Why didn't you just run away?" It's hard for anyone to say the right thing all the time, especially about something as shocking and frightening as sexual assault.

If you are a girl, you may be afraid to tell friends about an assault because you think you'll be looked on as "cheap," or at least as a fool who can't look after herself. If you are a boy, you may be afraid you'll be seen as gay or as a wimp. Everyone is afraid they'll be seen as strange and different now that they've been assaulted. Fears like these can, unfortunately, be justified because most people understand so little about sexual assault and are insensitive to it. Some teenagers refuse to go back to their old school after an assault because everyone knows about it. If you do go back, however, and you find that friends are making jokes at your expense or keeping away from you out of embarrassment, get help. You have suffered enough.

One of the best ways to get help is to arrange for a Rape Prevention Education program (see "Sources for Safety") to give a class in your school or community. In one suburban school, a girl who had been raped by a boy on campus reported the rape and was pressing charges. As a result, she was getting taunted by her schoolmates. The boys were making rape jokes, the girls were scared, and everyone was gossiping about her being a "slut" and having "asked for it." The teachers were so shocked at the way she was being treated that they called in S.A.F.E. (Safety and Fitness Exchange), a rape prevention program in New York. Everyone from the students to the teachers was grateful, for it not only taught them to take rape seriously, it showed them how to protect themselves.

If there are only a few students giving you a hard time, tell a teacher you trust (or ask your parents to). Those students should be taken aside and educated about sexual assault.

The best way to cope with friends after an assault is to tell only one or two who are very close to you and whom you trust. Dealing with school will be much easier if everyone doesn't know.

COPING WITH YOUR BOYFRIEND

If you are a girl and have a steady boyfriend, you'll probably want him to know about your assault. If your relationship is close, the secret will be too much to keep to yourself. And the assault will alter your feelings about sex, too, for a while.

Once you've told him a little about what happened to you, give him this book to read before you discuss it at length, especially chapter two, "Who Would Hurt You and Why." This will help him avoid the idea that you've been unfaithful, or that you're "spoiled" for him now. As unfair as these ideas are, a lot of people have them — especially boys. Explain that you'd like him to read the book because it'll help him understand what you've been through. If he reacts by getting furious at the attacker, tell him his fury isn't comforting you, it's just making you scared.

Suggest that he call up a rape crisis counselor to answer any questions he might have. A counselor can explain to your boyfriend that if he can prove that he respects and likes you as much as ever, and can show you that he doesn't blame you in any way, he can help you recover.

COPING FOR BOYS

If you are a boy, your problems after a sexual assault are unique. You have been the victim of a crime a lot of people don't even know exists, and you may rightly fear that people will see you as some kind of freak as a result. You may have questions like these:

• *Why did it happen to me instead of someone else? Do I look funny, weak, or helpless?* You were not picked on because of your looks or what you're like. You were picked on because you were there. Don't blame yourself for the assailant's problems.

• *Did the assault happen because I'm gay without knowing it?* No. Whether you are gay or not has nothing to do with the assault. Often an attacker will say, "You're just a faggot," but he's only trying to justify what he's doing. He probably says that to every male he assaults. An assault is no reflection of your sexuality.

• *Will the assault turn me gay?* No. A sexual assault cannot change a person's sexuality, even if it's committed by a man on a man. The most it will do is put you off making love or being touched by anyone, male or female, until you are over the shock. Don't worry — that is the usual reaction. It will pass.

• *Won't everyone think I'm gay if they find out?* There is a danger that people will think so because few understand that sexual assault is more about violence than sex. A male who molests another male is doing it to conquer and humiliate, not out of desire. Choose whom to tell very carefully.

• *I am gay and that's why this happened. I'm being punished.* Like many gay teens and adults, you might blame your sexuality for the assault. Because you may already feel like an outsider, like someone society doesn't approve of, it's easy to think that you were assaulted as some kind of punishment. "This shows how much society hates me," is one way people look at it. "This is what I get for living an 'abnormal' life-style," is another. A lot of gays and lesbians even feel deep down that they somehow deserved the assault because of their life-style, that they brought it on by being "different."

All victims of crime tend to blame themselves at times and it never makes sense. Much of the time, assailants neither know nor care about your sexual preferences; you are just an available victim to them. Don't take on a criminal's problems as your own. You are innocent of wrongdoing and you deserve as much sympathy and help as anyone who is ever assaulted.

If you are gay and have been assaulted, however, you should be careful in selecting people to turn to for help. You won't be helped much by someone who tends to blame you or is full of prejudice. Ask at a rape crisis center for a gay counselor, if they have one, and if you don't like the attitude of one counselor, demand another. You have a right to be helped, not hurt.

• *This only happened 'cause I'm a wimp, didn't it?* No. Strong, grown-up, athletic men get raped, too. Muscles and macho are no match for a gun, a knife, a group of guys, or even just being taken by surprise. You survived the attack, and that means you did the right thing.

• *How can I tell a friend or girlfriend about this?* You may worry that your friends will look down on you or see you as a freak if they find out, and that your girlfriend will see you as unmasculine or polluted by the assault. Your friends may be very shocked because they didn't even know boys can be sexually assaulted, so it's important to explain to them all you've learned here about assaults on males. Tell them it happens a lot, that it's an act of violence, not lust, and that you were victimized out of pure bad luck, not because of what you did or how you look. Tell them that 7 to 10 percent of the rapes of adults are committed on men by other men.

• *Am I ever going to be able to feel sexual again after this?* Yes, you are. But you may not be ready for a while. You need to get your self-respect back, and you need to be able to feel confident enough to relax. No one can feel sexual when they are scared, upset, and shocked.

• *I was assaulted by a woman. Shouldn't I be proud instead of upset?* No. A woman who molests a boy is after power and revenge, just like a man. She's using unfair advantages of authority and age to use your body and maybe hurt you, too. Sex should always be a matter of choice and love. You have a right to be angry and hurt.

Boys and men tend to shy away from rape counselors, because they are ashamed or they think rape crisis centers are only for women and girls. But counselors have seen plenty of boys and men. Some centers even have male counselors. Don't deny yourself the comfort, assurance, and advice you need.

COPING WITH SEX

If you're like anyone else who's been seriously assaulted, girl or boy, man or woman, you're wondering if you'll ever like sex again. Studies have found that assaulted adults and teenagers are able to enjoy making love again, but that it takes time. A sexual assault puts almost everyone off sex at first. You are not alone.

You may not want to be touched by anyone at all for a while. You may not even like your mother patting you, let alone anyone kissing you. So if your boyfriend or girlfriend pressures you to make love in some way and you aren't ready, don't. You need to heal before you can feel sexual again. You may have to say something like "I still like you, but I'm not ready yet. I need time to recover." And if they won't listen, you may have to stay away from them for a while. *Don't ever make yourself do anything sexual you don't want to* — it'll feel like being assaulted all over again.

If you don't have a steady boyfriend or girlfriend, you may not feel ready to start dating for a while. You'll find it hard to trust people you don't know or to be alone with a new date. Again, don't push yourself. Wait until you feel more secure, then maybe only go out with groups of friends for a while. It may take a month, it may take a year, but you will get back to normal.

If you were a virgin when you were assaulted, or you'd had very little sexual experience, you might be afraid that the experience will put you off sex for life. This doesn't have to be so. Karen, who has been quoted before, was a virgin when she was raped, yet listen to what she says about it now:

> Comparing rape to sex is like comparing a slug in the mouth to a kiss. When I started having real sex for the first time with my boyfriend a year after the rape, I discovered that the two experiences were so different I didn't even have to compare. The rape was horrible, but the lovemaking was beautiful.

To her, quite rightly, sex was an expression of love while the rape had been an act of violence. She came to think of the rape as an accident — nothing to do with her love life. If you can look at your assault that way too, you'll go a long way toward getting over it.

To help yourself keep the attack separate from your sexuality, remember the following:

• *Sexual assault is violence, not sex.* Assault is an act of hate, sex is an act of love.

• *Never hurry yourself to make love.* Take your time after an assault. Wait until you feel safe, loving, and secure. Wait until you feel real desire.

• *Never let anyone pressure you to make love.* Don't let a boyfriend, a date, a girlfriend, or even yourself make you kiss, hug, make out, or make love unless you really want to. That will feel too much like being assaulted again.

• *Remember your sexual rights and practice them.* If you

insist on the sexual rights outlined in chapter three, you'll help yourself enjoy a healthy and pleasant sex life.

PLACES TO CALL FOR HELP AFTER A SEXUAL ASSAULT

RAPE HOTLINE

The person who answers will tell you where to go and what to do, and will listen sympathetically to your story. You don't have to be a girl and you don't have to have been raped to use this service — it's for any victim of any kind of sexual assault. Rape hotlines are listed on the first page of your phone book or under "Rape" in the *R* section. Information will give you the number, too.

RAPE CRISIS CENTER

The rape hotline counselor will probably refer you to your nearest rape crisis center, which may be in a hospital. The counselors at these centers are trained to help boys and girls of your age. Often, they are survivors of sexual assault themselves, so they know how you are feeling. A counselor will go with you to the hospital and the police, if you want, but will never force you to report the assault or to seek medical help against your will. A counselor will also help you tell your family, if you'd like. *All treatment at the rape crisis center is confidential.*

JUVENILE CENTER

There may be a clinic or counseling center especially for teenagers in your area. See "Sources for Safety" at the back of this book, or ask at the rape crisis center.

THE POLICE: 911

You can call this emergency number or your local precinct number, available from Information. You should have this number taped to your phone in case of emergencies.

SELF-DEFENSE CLASSES

Later on, after the immediate problems of the assault are taken care of, you might want to take self-defense lessons. These not only make you stronger and more confident, they help you recover from an assault. See "Sources for Safety" for ways to find courses.

A sexual assault makes you feel terribly alone. Whether it was committed by a relative, friend, or stranger, it is shattering. It makes you feel picked out among everybody for special bad luck. Don't increase your loneliness by withdrawing into yourself or keeping the assault secret. You are not alone. There are millions of people who've been through what you have, and many of them want to help and comfort you. They want you to know the ways they've found of getting better. You are young and because of this you are resilient. It will take time and it will be difficult and painful, but if you seek help, you'll get over it.

Sources for Safety

If you ever get caught in an emergency, you won't want to be searching through phone books for the right number. Use this section to make a list of all the most important resources you might need. National numbers are provided, but you'll have to look up local numbers yourself. Keep the list where you can find it quickly, near the phone if possible. Some of the most important numbers, such as 911 and your local fire and police department, should be taped right to your phone anyway.

When 1-800 appears before a number, it means that number can be called free of charge. Some of these toll-free numbers will give you a local number where you can get immediate help.

SAFETY NUMBERS

Emergency Police and Fire   911

Your Local Police Precinct   _____

(Call Information or look up "Patrol Boro" or "Precincts" under "Police" in the *P* section of your City

Government Offices. They are in the colored pages at the back of your phone book.)

National Runaway Hotline   1-800-231-6949

Local Runaway Hotline   _____
(Look up "Runaway" in your phone book.)

Rape Hotline/Help   _____
(Look on the first page of your phone book or under "Rape" in the *R* section.)

Your Local Rape Crisis Center   _____
(Get from Rape Hotline or look under "Rape" in your phone book.)

Your Nearest Hospital   _____
(If you don't know the name, look up the names and addresses of hospitals under the Health Department heading in the City Government Offices section of the phone book.)

Al-Anon, Ala-Teen, or
Alcoholics Anonymous (AA)   _____
(Look up under "Alcoholics Anonymous" in the phone book.)

Child Abuse Hotline/Help   _____
(Look up on the first page of your phone book. If there is nothing there, look under "Social Services" in the City or State Offices section and find a subheading for "Children.")

Child Protection Services/Agency   _____
(Look under "Social Services" for children in the City or State Offices section of the phone book.)

Youth Hotline   _____
(Look under "Youth" in the phone book.)

Planned Parenthood/
Family Planning Clinic   _____
(Look under *P* or *F* in the phone book. A clinic can help with VD, birth control problems, and pregnancy.)

Teen Pregnancy Hotline _____
(If this isn't listed prominently in your phone book, call Planned Parenthood for information.)

Unplanned Pregnancy _____
(Call Planned Parenthood for information.)

Parents Anonymous _____
(Under *P* in the phone book. For abusive parents and their children. This number will put you onto help with stopping sexual or nonsexual abuse.)

Child Welfare League _____
(Under "Child" in the phone book or under "Social Services" in the City or State Government Offices section.)

Society for the Prevention of
Cruelty to Children 1-800-342-3720
(Call to report the abuse of a child or for advice on how to stop it.)

SELF-DEFENSE COURSES, RAPE PREVENTION EDUCATION, AND PLACES TO GO FOR HELP

If you need immediate help, call your local rape crisis center. If you want to find out about a self-defense course or a program that could be taught in your school or community, call or write to one of the organizations listed here or call your local YWCA or rape crisis center.

The following organizations specialize in providing help to teenagers.

CALIFORNIA

Child Assault Prevention (CAP) Training Center of Northern California
1495 Rose Street, No. 6
Berkeley, CA 94702-1255
Phone: (415) 528-1516

*Child Assault Prevention (CAP) Training Center of
Southern California*
5151 State University Drive
Los Angeles, CA 90032
Phone: (213) 224-3283

There are forty-six CAP training centers throughout California, so you can probably find one near you by calling or writing to the above addresses. CAP holds workshops for parents, teachers, and kids in and out of school, teaching that the young have the right to be "Safe, Strong and Free." They also provide bilingual services and teach in various cultural communities. CAP teaches students about sexual assault and sexual rights as well as physical self-defense.

CULVER CITY

Southern California Rape Prevention Study Program
Didi Hirsch Community Mental Health Center
4760 S. Sepulveda Boulevard
Culver City, CA 90230
Phone: (213) 390-6612/6691

Call this number to arrange for a speaker on child abuse prevention to come to your school or community center. Speakers will also address parent groups. *The Didi Hirsch Center also has a clinic for young victims of assault.*

LOS ANGELES

Adolescent Sexual Abuse Prevention Program
Brenda Lacy
Charles R. Drew Postgraduate Medical School
1621 East 120th Street
Los Angeles, CA 90059
Phone: (213) 563-5828

Brenda Lacy teaches a six-hour education program for teenage girls and boys on the prevention of sexual assault. The course is held during classroom time or on weekends in other community organizations.

OAKLAND

Oakland Men's Project
Paul Kivel and Alan Craton
Phone only: (415) 654-3015

This project specializes in addressing boys in junior high about sexual assault and child abuse. Presentations and workshops are held in schools.

SAN FRANCISCO

Brinkman & Associates
Phone only: (415) 661-4040

Trisha Brinkman teaches self-defense to women and girls.

SAN PABLO

After School Self-Defense
Rape Crisis Center of West Contra Costa
2000 Bale Road
San Pablo, CA 94806
Phone: (415) 237-0113

This program teaches girls and boys of all ages about sexual assault prevention. There is a six-hour program for grades 1–8, held in four after-school sessions; an eight-hour program for teenage girls and adult women, held in two four-hour sessions; and a special course taught for junior high boys by a man, held in two class periods.

MASSACHUSETTS

Street Smarts . . . An Ounce of Prevention
100 Fays Avenue
Lynn, MA 01904
Phone: (617) 592-3103

Samantha Koumanelis gives lectures on how to be street-smart and on self-defense.

MICHIGAN

Center for Sex Equity in Schools
SEB 1046
University of Michigan
Ann Arbor, MI 48109-1259
Phone: (313) 763-9910

This center will provide free information, resources, and technical assistance about sexual harassment and sex equality issues in schools. Its curriculum on sexual harassment in secondary schools is called "Who's Hurt and Who's Liable," and is for students, teachers, counselors, and administrators.

MINNESOTA

No Easy Answers: A Sexual Abuse Prevention Curriculum for Junior and Senior High Students
Cordelia Anderson Kent
Illusion Theater
528 Hennepin Avenue, Room 309
Minneapolis, MN 55403
Phone: (612) 339-4944

"No Easy Answers" is a twenty-lesson curriculum that is taught in five to fifteen class periods. The program goes into subjects such as incest, emerging sexuality, and date rape. The program can be performed anywhere in the country, and includes student handouts and instructions for teachers.

NEW YORK

The Door Center of Alternatives
618 Avenue of the Americas
New York, NY 10011
Phone: (212) 691-6161 (Monday to Friday, 2 P.M. to 10 P.M.)

The Door is a counseling center for adolescent victims of incest, rape, and other sexual assaults. It is also a service for runaways.

The Safety & Fitness Exchange (SAFE)
541 Sixth Avenue
New York, NY 10011
Phone: (212) 242-4874/5

SAFE offers self-defense training and workshops to teach children, teenagers, adults, and handicapped people about sexual assault prevention. It also offers lectures and programs for schools and community centers around the country.

OHIO

Child Assault Prevention (CAP) Project
National Assault Prevention Center
P.O. Box 02005
Columbus, OH 43202
Phone: (614) 291-2540

This is the national center for CAP, the program described under "California" above. CAP staff teach children and people who work with children, and will work in schools and community centers around the country.

WASHINGTON

BELLINGHAM

Coalition for Child Advocacy
SOAP Box Players
P.O. Box 159
Bellingham, WA 98227
Phone: (206) 734-5121 or 384-1470

The SOAP Box Players offers a workshop on sexual abuse, who does it, and how to avoid it.

SEATTLE

Alternatives to Fear
1605 17th Avenue
Seattle, WA 98122
Phone: (206) 328-5347

This organization, a project of several rape crisis centers in Washington State, offers a variety of programs for teenagers on self-defense and the prevention of sexual assault, rape, and acquaintance rape.

Personal Safety and Decision Making
Committee for Children
P.O. Box 51049
Seattle, WA 98115
No phone

This program teaches junior high students about how stereotypes and peer pressure can result in sexual exploitation. The curriculum is written to guide a teacher and can be presented in sessions lasting one, three, or five days.

Special Education Curriculum on Sexual Abuse and Exploitation
Comprehensive Health Education Foundation
20832 Pacific Highway South
Seattle, WA 98188
Phone: (206) 824-2907

This program is for handicapped students in secondary school grades. It teaches awareness and prevention of sexual exploitation.

BOOKS FOR TEACHING THE PREVENTION OF SEXUAL ASSAULT

- *Acquaintance Rape: Awareness and Prevention for Teenagers* by Py Bateman. (Pamphlet for individuals and classes. $4.00.)
- *Making It Work: A Community Action Plan for the Prevention of Teen Acquaintance Rape* by Alternatives to Fear project. (A guide for individuals and organizations on how to educate a community about acquaintance rape among teenagers. $3.50.)

To order these and similar booklets, call or write:

Alternatives to Fear
1605 17th Avenue
Seattle, WA 98122
Phone: (206) 328-5347

- *Personal Safety for Junior High.* A book for junior high teachers containing units on how to teach "Personal Safety," "Appropriate and Inappropriate Touching," "Assertiveness," and "Support Systems." ($20.) Available from:

Council on Child Sexual Abuse
P.O. Box 1357
Tacoma, WA 98401
Phone: (206) 593-6624

- *Sexual Abuse Prevention: A Study for Teenagers* by Marie M. Fortune. A booklet describing a five-session course on sexual abuse prevention for teenagers. For use by teachers and community leaders. (United Church Press, New York. $3.95.) Available in women's bookstores.

FILMS

- *The Party Game.* 16mm; color; 8 minutes. Shows how inadequate communication can lead to acquaintance rape.
- *The Date.* 16mm; color; 6½ minutes. Shows how sexual stereotyping can lead to acquaintance rape.
- *Just One of the Boys.* 16mm; color; 8½ minutes. Shows how stereotypes and peer pressure contribute to gang rape.
- *End of the Road.* 16mm; color; 9½ minutes. Teaches practical ways to prevent acquaintance rape.
- *A Night Out.* 16 mm; color; 10 minutes. The story of how a seemingly innocent date can turn into sexual assault, filmed in sign language for deaf teenagers.

The first four films are part of the Acquaintance Rape Prevention Series and come with a program guide, fact sheets, and posters. (*A Night Out* can be rented separately.) They can be rented for $125 a week plus $10 shipping from:

> O.D.N. Productions
> 74 Varick Street
> Suite 304
> New York, NY 10013
> Phone: (212) 431-8923

- *Better Safe Than Sorry.* 16mm; color; 14½ minutes. Deals with kidnapping, sexual abuse, murder, and self-protection. For children ages nine to fourteen. Also available in Spanish. Rental: $25.
- *Better Safe Than Sorry III.* 16mm; color; 19 minutes. Illustrates potentially dangerous situations for junior and senior high students, and how to avoid them. Also addresses male victimization. Rental: $25.

The above two films as well as other films about rape and safety are available from:

FilmFair Communications
10900 Ventura Boulevard
P.O. Box 1728
Studio City, CA 91604
Phone: (818) 985-0244 (Call collect
for information or orders.)

• *Boys Beware.* 16 mm; color; 14 minutes. Shows that boys can be victims of sexual assault and illustrates how to get out of a dangerous situation. Rental: $25.

• *Girls Beware.* 16mm; color; 12 minutes. Shows four typical situations that could be dangerous and how to avoid them. Rental: $25

These two films can be rented from:

Aims Media, Inc.
6901 Woodley Avenue
Van Nuys, CA 91406
Phone: 1-800-367-2467
In California or
Alaska: (818) 785-4111

• *Beyond Rape.* 16mm; color; 28 minutes. A film on all aspects of sexual assault for junior and senior high students. Rental: $70. Contact:

CORONET/MTI
108 Wilmot Road
Dearfield, IL 60015
Phone: 1-800-621-2131

• *Don't Get Stuck There.* 16mm; color; 15 minutes. Adolescents discuss their experiences of physical, sexual, and emotional abuse. Available *rent-free* from:

Boys Town Center
Boys Town Film Library
Boys Town, NE 68010
Phone: (402) 498-1595

Appendix for Parents

"Did you read that story about the little boy who was kidnapped and found murdered?" asked Lois, the mother of a six-year-old.

"I saw the headlines," Brigit, another mother, said with a shudder. "I just can't bear to read those stories."

"I know what you mean," said Lois. "Whenever I see anything about missing children or sexual abuse and any of that, I put it away. It's too depressing to read that stuff."

I heard this conversation in the home of a friend of mine. Both mothers were educated, urban people, well aware of the prevalence of child abuse. Because of my research on sexual assault, I suggested that they teach their kids the basics of self-protection. One mother put her hands over her ears. "Don't even tell me about it," she said. "I can't stand it."

Like so many of us, these women chose to hide from the problem rather than face it. The idea of a sexual assault, rape, or kidnapping happening to our sons and daughters is so terrifying that we often can't bear to think about it. Instead, we vow to keep an eye on our children every minute and we say to ourselves, "That won't happen to *my* child."

Refusing to face the problem will not, of course, help to protect anyone. In fact, assailants rely on the ignorance of children and teens to turn them into victims. As parents, we only have one choice: we have to protect our children as much as we can and, perhaps more important, teach them to protect themselves.

In my research, I've been impressed by how effectively children of all ages can protect themselves. I've seen little children break choke holds with their own small hands and I've heard accounts of older children successfully outwitting and escaping their would-be assailants. Most assailants of children know their victims; to entrap them, they rely less on violence than on the children's ignorance about sexual assault. That means that a child or teenager who knows what sexual assault is, and knows how to escape the danger *before* anything happens, has an excellent chance of avoiding assault.

There is another advantage you can give your children to help them protect themselves: your encouragement and support. This is particularly important when they are young teenagers — a time when they become especially vulnerable to sexual assault from both strangers and people they know. Young teenagers are still very dependent on their parents' opinions, even if they outwardly reject them, and if they know you approve of and encourage their attempts to learn about sex, its pleasures, and its dangers, they will feel much stronger. If you also support their attempts to learn self-protection — in the street, with people, on dates, at home — and actual self-defense, they will be doubly strong.

Here are some suggestions on how you can help your

son or daughter become independent in the safest and strongest of ways.

HOW TO HELP YOUR TEENAGER BE SAFER

• *Discuss family rules openly.* Tell your teenager clearly about where he or she can go, how late he or she can stay out, whom he or she can see. Make the rules clear and try to reach an agreement on their reasonableness. Teenagers need limits like these to define their world; without them they may be tempted to take personal risks merely to rebel.

• *Tell your teen that your primary concern is for his or her safety.* It must be made clear that these rules do not exist just to prove your authority.

• *Discuss what will happen if these rules are broken.* Make the consequences clear. Then, if it happens, stick to the rules yourself. Don't break promises.

• *Tell your teenager to call you* anytime *help is needed, with no fear of punishment.* Promise that you will come to the rescue with no questions asked, no anger, and no punishment, even if rules have been broken. This means that if your son is stuck in a bad part of town late at night, where he's been buying drugs, he should feel that he can call you to come get him rather than risking his safety by trying to get home alone. It means that if your daughter is alone with a boy when she'd told you she was with a girlfriend, and she's afraid he's going to assault her, she should feel able to call you. Later, after the fear has died down, you are certainly entitled to bring up the subject and express your concern about it. But keep your promises and remember that this kind of arrangement can be one of the most important safety valves your child can have.

• *Tell your child that you never want him or her to feel*

unable to tell you about a frightening event for fear of pun-ishment. So many kids keep their troubles secret from their parents for fear of punishment, thereby denying themselves help. Their trust in you should be more important than rules.

• *Explain that you'd rather be told about something like a sexual assault, even if it upsets you, than be kept in the dark.* Say you'd rather be upset but able to help than ignorant and unable to help.

• *Encourage your son or daughter to take a self-defense class.* These are available at the local YWCA and YMCA or from private organizations. (See "Sources for Safety.") Many organizations offer classes for the entire family.

• *Contact a Child Abuse Prevention Education group and arrange for a course to be taught in your community.* There is a list of these organizations under "Sources for Safety."

IF YOUR CHILD IS ASSAULTED

Studies have found that when an adolescent is sexually assaulted, his or her main concerns are, "Will my parents believe me?" "Will they be angry?" and "What will my friends think?" Anger at the assailant, or worries about health, pregnancy, and future sexuality, and concern about future safety seem to belong more to the victim's parents. Some researchers believe that the sexual assault of an adolescent actually upsets the parents more than the victim.

The assault of your child is without doubt one of the most shattering things that can happen to you. There is the agony of seeing someone young and innocent suffer from such a sordid crime. There is the terror that your child has been damaged for life. There is the terrible guilt at having failed to protect your child — your primary role as a parent. There is the wish that the assault had happened to you instead. Above all, there is the pain of seeing someone you love so much hurt so badly. The entire family will suffer, as well as the victim. You are what psychologists call "secondary victims."

The fact that you are so shattered by the assault of your child makes it more difficult to give the support he or she needs. Yet, your support is essential. As one researcher put it, "The adolescent's recovery depends largely on the support he or she receives."

"Well, of course I'll support my child and show my love," you might be thinking. "All I want to do is help." Yet, despite the best intentions of all parents, studies have found that parents are *not* that good at helping their children recover from sexual assault. One study of 122 male and female adolescent victims found that 41 percent of their parents blamed the child directly for the rape. Only 20 percent of those adolescents said their parents were consistently supportive. The other 80 percent said their parents overreacted, got too restrictive, got angry at them, or rejected or neglected them because of the family crisis the assault had triggered. Some victims have said their family's reactions were worse than the rape itself. As a policeman said,

> I've seen teenage girls come in who've been raped and their fathers are really mad at them. I've heard fathers say, "I told you this was going to happen if you hang around with that crowd."

That's as unfair as saying to a mugging victim, "I told you not to walk home with a wallet in your pocket."

In order to avoid making mistakes that will increase your child's suffering, remember these facts:

• *Sexual assault is never the victim's fault.* If your son or daughter was taking a risk, breaking a rule, or being careless, he or she was being a normal adolescent, not inviting an assault. Kids do those things all the time, but most of them don't get assaulted. Your child was horribly unlucky and it isn't fair to blame him or her for it. Many people tend to blame the victims of a crime — "They deserved it 'cause they did something stupid." Try to be realistic and supportive instead.

• *Despite myths to the contrary, very few kids make up stories about being sexually assaulted.* Often they are too ignorant to even know that such things happen. In any case, the shame and embarrassment attached to the subject is too great for most people to voluntarily immerse themselves in. You may want to disbelieve your child out of a need to deny the horror of it, but doing so will only make your child feel worse.

• *Sexual assault is a terrible tragedy, but kids are resilient.* With your support and understanding, your child has more chance of recovering than many an adult.

HOW TO HELP YOUR CHILD RECOVER

Right after the assault, follow these steps:

• *If your teenager tells you about an assault, be grateful you were told at all.* Many kids never do, so that means your teenager trusts you. Say something like "I'm really glad you told me — that was brave."

• *Assure your child that you love, respect, and believe him or her.* Say something like "I believe you, I love you, and I'm going to do all that I can to help you feel better."

• *Tell your teenager that you know the assault wasn't his or her fault.* Without such assurance children are prone to blame themselves.

• *If you cannot hide your anger, direct it at the assailant.* Assure your child with words like "I'm proud of you and I'm sad for you, but I'm not angry at you." Try to let off your anger elsewhere.

• *Ask if he or she wants to go to the hospital, a rape crisis center, and the police right after the assault or later.* It's important that you offer to be there, but let your child make the decision about when and whether to go. Because a sexual assault robs the victim of all sense of control and self respect, it's very important to let your child make decisions right away.

After the initial crisis:
• *Remember that you will need sympathy, too.* Don't try to be a superparent, or else something's going to crack. Let yourself talk to someone else about the assault and your feelings, a counselor if need be. But around your child, concentrate on his or her needs.
• *Suggest contacting a rape crisis center for counseling.* Don't force your child to do it, but if you think it's needed as time goes on, gently suggest it again. Offer to participate in the sessions but don't insist.
• *Don't change the rules about when and where your child can go now.* A teenager in particular needs to know that the assault hasn't infringed on his or her attempts to grow up.
• *Don't keep treating your child as special or fragile.* Like any victims of assault, teenagers need to feel that life can be normal again, that they aren't different, and that they aren't responsible for disrupting their family's life.
• *On the other hand, don't force your child to get back to normal immediately.* Your child may need a few days out of school, or a light on at night, or not to be left alone. Be sensitive to these needs. LET YOUR CHILD MAKE THESE DECISIONS.
• *If the victim is a boy, he'll need special reassurance.* He may be terribly shocked by having fallen victim to a crime he didn't even know existed. He (and you) may think, "I thought only girls were raped. What's weird about me?" Assure him that the sexual assault of boys

is not unusual, that nothing is wrong or different about him, and that his masculinity is not compromised by it.

• *Expect your child to go through a difficult period.* Normal reactions to sexual assault include insomnia, nightmares, phobias, and reluctance to see friends. These reactions might start immediately after the assault, but they might not come up until several days or weeks later. The victim is also likely to go through a phase of denying that the assault is traumatic. As this mother said,

> After my daughter was raped when she was fifteen, she handled the police and the hospital all on her own. But then she said she was over it, didn't need counseling, and didn't want to talk about it. It's been a year now and she still won't talk about it. She seems okay, but I'm not sure.

Maybe the girl *is* over it — some people do recover quickly — but it isn't such a good sign that she won't talk about it. Often the trauma comes out in seemingly unrelated ways, like recurrent headaches or stomach troubles or other physical ills. If your child is having symptoms like these and is denying the assault, get help from a doctor and suggest counseling.

• *Reassure your teenager that reactions like those described above are normal and happen to everyone after a sexual assault.* Your child may fear that he or she is going crazy.

• *Keep telling your child that you love him or her.* Children often feel extremely unlovable after a sexual assault. They need to know they are still attractive and nice.

• *Emphasize that you respect your child.* Adolescents become especially concerned with their image after something as damaging as an assault. They need to feel proud of having survived such an ordeal. They need to know that they are still worthy of respect.

• *Don't drop the subject of the assault forever.* If you do, it'll become a forbidden subject in the family, which will make it impossible for your teenager to ask questions about it or talk about it when he or she needs to. Every now and then, at appropriate moments — after a nightmare, following a violent movie, or when your child is upset — say that you would like to talk about it and would be happy to listen.

• *Expect family tensions to result from this trauma.* There will be fights and explosions. You and your spouse might blame each other for the assault. Your other children may get jealous of the attention the victim is getting, or feel guilty that it didn't happen to them. The family may be angry at the victim for bringing on this crisis. If things get out of hand, consider family counseling through a rape crisis center.

• *If you are a father, don't withdraw from the family with the sense that sexual assault is a woman's problem.* Your respect and love for the victim, boy or girl, are doubly important now. You can supply the much-needed role model of a man who is gentle and understanding, not violent like the assailant. You are largely responsible for proving that not all men are bad.

• *If your son or daughter is miserable at school, discuss what can be done about it.* Ask your teenager if you can discuss the problem with the teachers. Perhaps you could bring in a rape education program to help improve the students' attitude. It may be necessary to change schools.

HOW TO RECOGNIZE THAT YOUR CHILD HAS BEEN ASSAULTED

Many teenagers never tell their parents about an assault, even when they are on good terms with them. They don't want to upset you, they are afraid you'll get too restrictive and overprotective, they value their privacy too much, or they are confused and bewildered about why it happened. Some think it's their own fault and that they don't deserve sympathy. As a result, they become lonely and depressed. Here are some symptoms that might indicate a sexual assault. If you see any of them, ask your child gently if he or she has been hurt by someone, is scared about something, or is upset. Make sure you say, "I won't be angry because I know it's not your fault, but I want to know so I can help."

- *Any extremely sudden change of behavior.* This can include not going out anymore, not coming home, not eating, or eating too much.
- *Sudden depression, quietness, or explosions of anger.*
- *Rapid gain or loss of weight.*
- *Sudden uncharacteristic obsessions with sex, or, in a boy, with homosexuality.*
- *Abrupt display of delinquent behavior.* This includes taking drugs, staying out late, picking fights, cutting school, flunking courses — anything that reflects a sudden loss of self-esteem or tendency toward self-punishment.
- *Sudden aversion to a certain person or place.*
- *Dramatic reaction of fear or distress at a violent or sexual scene in a movie.*
- *Nightmares, crying spells, insomnia.*
- *Dressing differently, such as wearing many layers of clothes.* Kids who've been sexually assaulted often try to cover their bodies up as if to hide — this is not the same as trying to look fashionable.
- *Washing obsessively or not at all.*
- *Deliberately hurting him- or herself.*

Of course, these symptoms don't necessarily mean your child has been sexually assaulted, but they certainly mean something is wrong. Ask what the matter is and give your child the number of a local youth hot-line or rape crisis center.

If your teenager gets VD or becomes pregnant, con-sider the possibility of sexual assault. Say "I won't get angry because you couldn't help it, but I want to know if anyone forced you to have sex." Don't punish your child for what's happened even if he or she wasn't as-saulted — the consequences have been bad enough.

If your teenager *was* assaulted, follow the sugges-tions given earlier and make sure you say you are glad he or she told.

ASSAULT BY A FAMILY MEMBER

If your son or daughter has been sexually assaulted, be prepared for the possibility that the assailant is some-one in your family. It could be your brother, your fa-ther, your husband, your son. It will be very difficult for your child to tell you this, so as painful as it is for you to hear, you must be as supportive as you can. Be-lieving your child and protecting him or her will, in the long run, help the whole family, the offender included. Here are some suggestions to help you handle this tragic event:

• *Protect your son or daughter — and other children — from further assaults.* If you can find a way of doing this with-out sending them away from home, so much the bet-ter. Stay with them if you can. Leave with them if you must. Don't leave any of your children alone with the offender. Arrange for a friend or relative to stay with them if you must go to work.

• *Let your child go to school and have as normal a life as possible, as long as it doesn't put him or her in danger.* Your child needs to feel that life can go on normally.

• *Confront the offender.* If you can't do it on your own, for fear of violence or any other reason, think of whose help you can enlist. Other family members? Friends? Your priest, rabbi, or minister? A therapist?

• *If the offender denies it and accuses the child of lying, side with your child.* If you don't believe your child, his or her suffering will double.

• *Seek help.* Call your local rape crisis center, Parents Anonymous, or a child protection service for counseling about what to do. Some areas have a Parent Helpline listed in the phone book for cases like this. Some also have Domestic Violence and Child Abuse hotlines in the front of the phone book under "Community Services."

• *Don't try to cope with everything on your own.* Discovering that someone you love is a child molester is deeply shattering. You deserve all the comfort and counseling you can get.

• *Call the police.* If the offender is a danger to any of your children or you, call the police. An arrest or even a warning will stop the abuse, at least temporarily. Many families don't want to take legal action against the offender. Perhaps the offense seems too mild; perhaps you love the offender too much. You may be tempted to believe this was an aberration and will never happen again, but be warned — child molesters rarely do it only once. Don't forget your child, out of the wish to protect the offender or to deny that this horrible thing has happened. Help your child get free from the assaults and help the offender stop committing them if you can, but above all don't let things continue as they are. If you do, your son or daughter will be scarred for life.

If you can inform yourself about the realities of sexual assault — what it is, who commits it, how it affects people — you can do a great deal to help your child be safer. And that is giving your child strength that will last a lifetime.